FROM HURT
TO *Hope*

by *Farrar Moore*

with *Sheryl Cook & Betty Wolstenholm*

Caring
RESOURCES

Published in Nashville, Tennessee by Crowned Image Publishing

www.crownedimagepublishing.com

with Caring Resources
818 Shadowstone Place
Nashville, TN 37220
www.caringresources.com

Special discounts are available on quantity purchases by corporations, associations, and others. Orders by US trade bookstores and wholesalers—for details, contact the publisher at the website above.

Photography: Sarah Siegand

Printed in the United States of America

Forth Edition, 2020
ISBN: 978-1-946622-10-5

Contents

1 *Hurt*

That whole unbelievable year was permeated with a despair that seemingly had no end. My mother was dying. I vacillated between feelings of sadness, guilt, heaviness, and fear. Some consulting work I had spent months doing, although initially well-received, had been abandoned, pushing my buttons that triggered feelings of rejection and insignificance. My husband, Charlie, not a fan of change, was agonizing over taking a risk with a new job. We both were struggling with uncertainty—what did God want us to do? Our daughter was planning a Christmas wedding, and if you have ever been a mother-of-the-bride, you know the energy, time, and emotion that goes into that role. Hard things often seem to come in groups—like pileups on the freeway in the fog. There were other, less overwhelming stresses, but these surface easily in my memory.

The wedding, the bright spot in the dreary year, was the Sunday before Christmas. The bride, a treasure, exuded radiance. Every glance at her glow was delightful. We had a wonderful time basking in the moment with family and friends, both old and new. There was a lot of laughter, good conversation, warm fuzzies, and delicious food. By the time the last of the guests had gone home, our hearts were full; and our feet were screaming. It had been a wonderful day!

The next day was definitely a crashing day—we were too tired to think. With our bodies molded into the sofa, we talked to each other about the people we had seen and those with whom we had reconnected, the beautiful flowers, the cute children, and that wonderful cake. By afternoon though, we were hungry and decided to go to a new Mexican restaurant that we thought our other daughter's boyfriend might enjoy.

It was about ten miles away. We thought it wouldn't be too crowded since it was still early on a Monday night.

So, the four of us headed across the south end of town for dinner. It was about five o'clock, already dark on a chilly December evening. We were driving down a four-lane road—lots of cars and lots of lights. Suddenly, there was a sickening impact—the right corner of our car had hit something and thrown it up into the windshield! It was horrible! Everything suddenly shifted to slow motion. What do we do? Where do we go? Emotional and physical paralysis overwhelmed us. After what seemed like a lifetime, but actually only a few seconds, the car stopped on the shoulder of the road almost under its own direction.

With the sound of gravel under the tires, I jerked back to reality. Car doors flew open. I ran back to the limp body of a young teen in a thin, white shirt lying on the shoulder of the road. I was the first one to reach her. I laid my hand gently on her back, praying continually. My heart knew she was dead, but my mind prayed, "Jesus, won't you please breathe life back into her?"

But I knew she was gone—not coming back. I had a strong feeling that she knew God, that she was with Him at that very moment.

Others began to gather, patrons of a market, and apartment dwellers— siblings who had also been running across the street encircled us. I had to move. I knew my presence was inappropriate as her family came around her. I got up and walked back to the grass next to the car. Feelings of horror, disbelief, gut-wrenching pain seemed to hover over the growing group. People came out of nearby apartments with blankets and prayers—compassionate hearts and comforting hands. It seemed to take so long for the ambulance and the police to come. Tape measures, yellow tape, a white tennis shoe, glares, questions, prayers, hugs. Waiting. When the ambulance finally left, there was no siren.

Friends came, ours and theirs. What would we have done without them? God, Jesus, the Holy Spirit, angels—they were all there. We couldn't have kept breathing without Him. But the pain—it was there, too—a dense cloud that almost smothered the breath out of our bodies. Eventually, we were driven home, probably close to ten o'clock—no food, no words, no plan. Should we eat? Go to bed? Was sleep an option? Time suddenly seemed to be a missing dimension—too slow, too fast.

Somehow, sometime it got to be morning. The initial silence was calm and awkwardly deceptive. Maybe if we were still and quiet, the time would go by until it all just went away. Would this nightmare ever end? Friends came at just the right time. The darkened room didn't keep them from coming to the bed—"Get up, it was an accident."

Then it was night again, and then another morning. We seemed to be stuck in a permanent replay of the video, but in some surreal way the days kept right on going. The city kept on living. There were lots of calls. One woman asked, "Were your lights on?" Would the correct answer change the video? Yes, the lights were on. "Was alcohol involved?" No, no alcohol. "Were you speeding?" No, the speed was under the limit. What difference would any of that have made? This thirteen-year-old girl was gone; there was an empty seat when her family gathered. Her mother would never plan a wedding for her, with her.

Our wedding—there was no more talk of it—no looking at pictures, no reliving of the pleasant memories of that event. A bigger event, one of weightier consequence had displaced the wedding.

Depression and then anger began to fill every little gap in my emotional being. I wasn't angry at anyone or anything specifically, but I certainly directed it at whomever or whatever was in front of me. Ironically, I don't remember being angry at God. I do remember thinking that He could have changed the circumstances. A green light could have been red; a red light, green. There could have been more traffic, less traffic.

God could have changed things. But—He didn't. I did not believe this tragedy was His design; but I did and do believe that as I cooperated with Him, He would work His purposes for His glory out of this horrible circumstance. And somehow, He would work everything for my good, for Charlie's good, and for the good of the family with the missing daughter and sister. I trusted Him. I believed Him. I chose to cooperate with Him.

But, I was still angry.

One particular Sunday morning, I was feeling especially low. I really needed to talk, but no one asked me the right questions, which in my mind would have given me permission to talk. Everyone just wanted me to be okay again. So, I kept all my pain and emotion stuffed. I recall one woman saying to me, "Christians everywhere are being attacked right now." That was a fact that brought me no consolation. I think she wanted me to know that I was not alone in my suffering. I could trust God. However, the thought that came to me in that moment was that if I had a broken arm and a million other people had broken arms, my pain wouldn't be any different. My broken arm would hurt just the same as if I were the only one hurting. If I really believed God, if I really trusted Him, would I only be happy and peaceful, not ever angry, depressed, or sad? If I was angry, depressed, or sad, did it mean that I really didn't trust Him? And, if that was true, if I didn't really believe, should I add guilt and shame to the anger, depression, and sadness? At the moment, I was just angry, and I didn't know what to do!

?

What is often the reaction by people—even in the church— when Christians are angry or depressed?

When have you been angry or depressed?

What were you feeling?

In the midst of that Sunday of my simmering anger, this Scripture came to mind, "Weep with those who weep." Whoa. I repeated it in my mind over and over. What did that mean? How did that apply now? I thought back over my life and realized that in my times of weeping, what I had heard most often were all the reasons I should not be weeping. Wasn't that what I did with my daughters, my friends? If I could just help them understand some fact or some truth, then they would realize that grieving was unnecessary. Really?

Where was that verse anyway? I found it—Romans 12:15. In my Bible the heading of the chapter read *Christian Behavior*. Paul was telling the Christians in Rome how to treat each other—love each other, be patient, cry with each other, rejoice with each other. Wow! We'd certainly missed the boat on that "cry" part. I reread that chapter several times. Paul was serious. I thought about all the hurting Christians and then all the rest of the hurting people. If God wanted us to weep with each other, then certainly that was what Jesus was doing for me. He was weeping with me.

A flood of comfort washed over me as I pictured Jesus crying with me, feeling how I felt, integrating Himself in my emotion. Jesus weeping with me—not speaking, just loving me; not telling me how to feel—or how I shouldn't feel—just feeling with me. He knows me. He feels with me. He really loves me!

? How do those closest to you respond when you express emotions of grief?

How did your parents respond to your emotion?

After experiencing His love and comfort, I wanted Jesus to teach me how to "weep with the weeping." What if I and the Church participated in weeping with those who are grieving? We would be a safe place for the wounded, the weary. What an impact we could make. I wanted to be that kind of Church. "Blessed are those who mourn, for they will be comforted."[1] Jesus actually said those words in His discourse on life principles in Matthew 5. He certainly must have thought it was important because it was the second beatitude in His "Sermon on the Mount."

*Mourning—crying, grieving—*is precious to Jesus. He can bless me with His comfort if I am willing to mourn. Why is it so difficult to mourn? Have I incorrectly equated mourning with weakness? Actually, it takes a lot of strength to grieve. Weakness? No. After all, God, Jesus, and the Holy Spirit grieve, too—with no weakness implied or even considered!

? If you refuse to mourn, do you take yourself out of the reach of His comfort?

At the beginning of His ministry, Jesus was teaching in the synagogue in Nazareth. He opened the scroll and read from Isaiah 61. "The Spirit of the Lord is upon Me because He has anointed Me to preach the gospel to the poor. He has sent Me to *heal the brokenhearted*; to proclaim liberty to the captives and recovery of sight to the blind; to set at liberty those who are oppressed; to proclaim the acceptable year of the Lord."[2] Then, He rolled up the scroll and gave it back to the attendant. After a very pregnant pause, He told all those listening that they were seeing the fulfillment of that Scripture. Jesus, the fulfillment, was standing right there in front of them!

Isn't it amazing that healing broken hearts ranks so high in the purposes of Jesus? Actually, it is only second to preaching the gospel in Isaiah's prophetic list. Why has it ranked so low with us? I can learn to mourn and receive His comfort, and He will heal my heart—how wonderful!

As I began to listen and look to Jesus, I realized it was more than just the accident that had broken my heart. What exactly did I need to grieve? I began to realize that I had a lifetime of experiences and circumstances that had caused wounds, cracks, fractures, and deep gashes in my heart. The door I was about to open wasn't just the door to a closet of emotion; it was the door to a long, winding hallway of doors. Each loss I had experienced was a door that I must open in order to adequately mourn. I had to mourn to receive His healing. But what really counted as loss? What label was on each one of those doors?

Loss happens every time what is or what I experience is different from what I expected or what I wanted.

After this definition of loss, do any experiences come to mind as losses that never seemed like loss before?

One spring I was in Atlanta and visited North Point Community Church. I heard Andy Stanley talking about the first few verses in James 4 from a challenging perspective. Addressing the "wars among you" he asked, "Why do you have all that inner turmoil?" According to James, it is because you don't get what you want. Basically, it is our definition of loss: *what you have, where you are, what you are doing is not what you wanted or expected.*

Russell Friedman and John James at the Grief Recovery Institute teach that loss is cumulative—it all adds up from day one. I am born with an emotional vessel in my heart—in the core of my being. It's empty, or almost empty, at birth. I think that changes pretty quickly. My emotional cup begins to fill with emotion that is left unresolved. This unresolved, unaddressed emotion stays in my cup. This unprocessed emotion is generating and formulating emotional reactions and responses for future loss-bringing experiences. What a setup!

I was not taught how to process loss. Consequently, I was oblivious that I needed to teach or model processing loss to my children. How about you? Losing a doll, watching a quarter roll into a street drain, watching dad drive away, ripping a new coat, a best friend moving away, the death of grandma, being very sick, not making the team, striking out, dropping the pass, losing an election, feeling left out or ignored, being misunderstood or ridiculed, the divorce of parents, abuse, injury, rejection—the loss list can go on and on. Losses just keep happening. My emotional cup, and probably yours, was full to the brim by the time I was eleven or twelve. And, I had a good childhood, loving parents, and good friends. This may not have been your experience.

Picture that vessel with all that unprocessed emotion swirling around—each emotion keeping its own properties, but all of them mixed up together. The vessel is full with no room for any more emotion without some reaction. Soon it is overflowing, over-reacting with inappropriate responses to circumstances—responses that really don't seem to make sense. It's difficult to identify each separate, individual emotion.

My presenting emotion—the overflow—always seemed to look like anger. But, there were so many more emotions in my cup. When something happened—a loss, the accident—it felt like that whole glass full of emotions was thrown in my face. And, the only emotion I identified or felt was anger. I was ashamed of my emotion, and that shame kept it stuffed. I even denied that it was there.

A vessel full of unprocessed emotion blocks my sensitivity to the Holy Spirit, which robs me of peace, joy, and hope. Unresolved emotions from disappointments, losses, and hurts weigh me down, distract me, and hinder my progress. When this weight is coupled with sin, I remain too tired and too overwhelmed to hope. A full cup keeps me from being who God created me to be, doing what God purposed for me to do.

But, is there hope? Absolutely! I can take the lid of shame off that vessel. I can look inside, pull out an emotion, identify it, let God's light shine on it, process it, and let the healing power of Jesus Christ dissipate it! The same is true for you!

2 *Suffer*

God devoted the whole book of Job in the Old Testament to responding to loss. I'm sure you remember the story of Job, a man of great wealth, reputation, and prominence—at least initially. Then without warning, a servant stumbled in, crying about raiders murdering servants and stealing all of Job's oxen and donkeys. Before Job could even hear any details, another man ran in to tell of a fire that had completely consumed Job's sheep and the servants caring for them. Before Job could respond to that news, a third report came of more raiders—the camels and servants—gone. The awareness of financial devastation had not hit when yet another, the fourth messenger came, bringing the worst news of all—a fierce wind had collapsed the house where all of Job's children were celebrating. They were all dead—they and the servants with them. Only the four messengers bearing the news of the horrendous events had survived.[1]

Job, in anguish, tore his robe and shaved his head, physically expressing his pain. Then, Job responded in worship, "The Lord gives and the Lord takes away; Blessed be the Name of the Lord."[2] He spoke the truth. He knew and understood what was true. Regardless of his circumstances, he knew that God is Almighty and must be worshiped for Who He is.

? What are some good "religious" answers to adversity that you have heard or given?

But Job's heart was breaking, and speaking the truth was an intellectual activity—brain-related, not heart-related. Job was dealing with the pain in his mind. Like Job, we attempt to sooth our own heartbreak with truth. We think that if we really believe, then the "bad" emotional response will just go away. If we just have the correct spiritual response, our emotions will appropriately follow suit.

Life couldn't get any worse—but, it could and did. Job lost his health—he had painful boils all over his body, head to toe. His wife, also in shock and unbelievable grief, advised Job to just curse God and die. She was probably craving death herself. But Job, still hoping that knowing the truth would keep his heart from breaking, answered, "Shall we indeed accept good from God, and shall we not accept adversity?"[3] Maybe this answer seemed curt or spiritual to his wife—another statement of truth—but the emotion that seemed to be in opposition to truth was welling up inside. Job was trying to keep his response at an intellectual level, but the question at the end of his statement indicated that he perhaps was beginning to rationalize. He didn't know what to do with, or how to explain, the emotion that was about to erupt.

You may remember that at this point Job's three friends met to go together to mourn with Job and comfort him.[4] The severity of Job's condition, obvious even from a distance, provoked their own mourning. They were drawn to his side, where for seven days and nights they sat with him—no one speaking. Seven days, wailing, sobbing, perhaps at times arm-in-arm or in embrace, with no words. What was Job thinking about during those seven days? That he would never again see his sons and daughters? Remembering special times with each of them? Realizing his lost influence among his countrymen? Or, was he so wracked with pain that he really couldn't think at all?

Job's statements of truth and rationalization had been unable to stop the tsunami of emotion that had taken over his being. "After this, Job opened his mouth and cursed the day of his birth, 'Why did I not die at birth? Why did I not perish when I came from the womb?'"[5] Pure emotion!

?

When was a time in your life that your pain was so great
that you had to be honest about your emotions?

Job's friends, Eliphaz, Bildad, and Zophar, were horrified by this out-
burst of emotion. Emotional honesty just didn't fit with their theology.
Eliphaz arrogantly stated the obvious—at least obvious to him and his
buddies, "Is not your reverence your confidence? And the integrity of
your ways your hope? Remember now, who ever perished being innocent? Or where were the upright ever cut off?" In this Scripture (Job
4:6–7), Eliphaz said that man's confidence and hope are in his own
ability to "do right." Eliphaz was expressing the common "spiritual" belief that only those who do not "do it right" will suffer. So this religious
perception is that if your circumstances are not good, then you have
not been good. Bottom line: *do good, get good; do bad, get bad.*

Sadly, this is the paradigm of many of us who call ourselves Christians
today. If this is your religious perception of life, you will always have a
need to blame; and you will be critical and judgmental of anyone in difficult circumstances.

Romans 5:1–5 indicates a completely different, irrational, but godly
system: "Therefore, having been justified by faith, we have peace with
God through our Lord Jesus Christ, through whom also we have access
by faith into this grace in which we stand, and rejoice in hope of the
glory of God. And not only that, but we also *glory in tribulations*,
knowing that *tribulation (suffering) produces perseverance*;
and *perseverance, character; and character, hope.* Now hope
does not disappoint, because the love of God has been poured out in
our hearts by the Holy Spirit who was given to us." (emphasis, mine)

Hope cannot exist without character; character cannot exist without perseverance; and perseverance cannot exist without suffering. Suffering is purposeful. In fact, James 1:2–4 says, "My brethren, count it all joy when you fall into various trials, knowing that the testing of your faith produces patience. But let patience have its perfect work, that you may be perfect and complete, lacking nothing." Remember that joy and happiness are two different emotions. Sadness from adverse circumstances can displace happiness. But joy, that deep, penetrating awareness of who I am and Whose I am, and where I am going, cannot be easily displaced. As joy grows and deepens, it remains, regardless of the gravity of other painful emotions.

? Can you see purpose in your past suffering?

A rule of thumb to assess your belief system might be your response to the negative circumstances of another. Is your initial response, either mentally or verbally, a judgment or criticism of prior actions or non-actions that could have led to these circumstances? The teenager injured in an accident—he must have been speeding, or drinking; his parents must not have disciplined him. The young woman with cervical cancer—she had been sleeping around; her nutrition was terrible. The couple who lost their house—they just had to have what they wanted; they probably never tithed. The older man who had to have his leg amputated—he never could get his diabetes under control; he was so undisciplined.

Do bad—get bad? We see this "religious" paradigm in John 9:1–12, when Jesus and His disciples passed a man who had been blind from birth. "Rabbi, who sinned, this man or his parents, that he was born blind?" Jesus answered, "Neither this man nor his parents sinned, but that the works of God should be revealed in him."

What was Jesus' initial, reactive response to the pain of another? Pain that may have been the result of that person's own sin? Or the consequences of someone else's sin? Or things that just happened? We do live in a fallen world, after all. I want my "knee-jerk" response to be like that of Jesus—compassion. Jesus was fully truthful AND fully compassionate. Compassion *and* Truth! Compassion should be the *first responder* to pain; then Truth can follow as led by the Holy Spirit!

Jesus—
fully Truth
AND
fully compassion!

There is not a FORMULA that we can apply: *bad things do not equal a bad person!* Regardless of the source of my pain—my sin (which definitely causes pain for others as well as for me); the sin of another (the consequence of another's sin affects me); things that just happened (we do live in a fallen world)—*in **all** my circumstances, God cares about me!*

Your life is about *relationship* with Him—not performance, not circumstances, not failures, not successes. God does not consider the source of your pain in determining His care for you. *The depth of His love and His care are steadfast.*[6]

Regardless of the source
of my pain,
in ALL my
circumstances
God cares about me!

Okay, God. I can believe that even if my pain is my own fault, the result of my sin or bad judgment or error in performance, You really care about me—but look—my heart is *still* broken. I can't know enough or believe enough to put it back together. It feels as though I'm standing with my nose right up against the bricks on the outside corner of a big, municipal building.

I'm only aware of the hard, rough bricks—my pain. I'm so close to it that I can't focus on anything else. I have no perspective. I don't know what's down the street on either side, what's behind me, what's going on in any other place—just the one square foot where I'm standing. I'm only conscious of *myself* and *my* pain.

In Psalm 86:11–12, David expressed it this way, "Teach me Your way, O Lord; I will walk in Your truth; unite my heart to fear Your name. I will praise You, O Lord my God, with all my heart, and I will glorify Your name forevermore." Now this may seem a little stretching for you, but if David had to ask God to unite his heart, then it must have been broken. David had some wisdom here that we don't often have. He realized that with a broken heart, he could not wholeheartedly praise God and glorify His name. With a broken heart, he could not fear God.

I grew up in a Christian, church-going, Bible-believing home. I knew that fear in relation to God meant an awe, a reverence for God—His power, His omnipotence—God Most High. But that word *fear* was just a little difficult for me. It had some experiential connotation that gave me a feeling of always being at a stiff arm's length from God. Thankfully, God in His grace, gave me two words to use instead of fear—words that I could get my arms around: *focus* and *perspective*.

My heart's desire is to focus on God, relate to Him in every situation and experience. So when my heart is broken and my nose is up against that brick wall, I find it impossible to focus on Him. Have you ever found yourself brokenhearted and trying to focus on God through reading His Word or through prayer? You read the same verse over and over again but are not really reading it. Your mind cannot stay on the words. You read the words, but your mind never seems to take them in. You begin to pray, but after only seconds your mind has a mental video of a painful event or conversation replaying—over and over again. You can't focus on God, and you can't really focus on anything but your pain.

In my brokenheartedness with my nose up against the bricks, I have no perspective. In this place of pain, *everything* is about *me*! Whatever is happening to anyone, anywhere, I can only see how it affects me and makes my life more difficult. In fact, in my "nose-against-the-bricks" state, it seems that *everything* is happening just to annoy, frustrate, or harm *me*.

Road rage is a perfect example of lack of perspective. It is as if the guy in the green SUV has been waiting for hours on a side street—waiting for me to drive by so that he could pull out in front of ME. It's personal. It's an attack. It's all about *me*. Oh, to have God's perspective. I want to seek His perspective in every circumstance.

Back to the brick wall—here I stand, mired in the emotion of circumstances, brokenhearted, nose against the bricks with no focus, no perspective, in great need of Jesus and His healing. With my left eye, I peer down the wall a little way—the past. Regret, *if only I, if only he, I should have, she could have, if only, if only, if only.* That mental video of an event, an interaction, a period of time, just keeps replaying. Maybe the next time I hit replay, something different will happen. But it doesn't. It's the same ending every time, over and over again.

> In my place of pain,
> it's all
> —everything—
> is about me.

With my right eye, I anticipate or predict the future, maybe ten years—or ten minutes—scripting or calculating. I think about what I'm going to say, or what I'm going to do; what the other person is going to say, or what the other person is going to do. I forget that no one else has my script—a setup for disappointment (at best) or a relationship altering blowup.

I've been known to do a lot of scripting even when I wasn't brokenhearted. I remember the first year that both of my children were off at college. I was really anticipating a joyful Thanksgiving. I started planning—scripting—early. I didn't know I was scripting. In my mind it was just good planning. The end of the recap would read: "and a good time was had by all." I would prepare everyone's favorite dish: mashed potatoes, sweet potatoes, peas, green beans, turkey for the turkey person, ham for the ham person, etc. They would be so appreciative—glowing commendations, hugs. They would be so thankful for my efforts that the cleanup would be a community effort—a simultaneous dish-washing and sing-along. How wonderful! Then we would watch a little football and play Scrabble or charades. Maybe we could even look at old pictures. What a day!

Can you see the problem here? My daughters and husband and extended family had totally different scripts. I failed to make copies of my script to hand out with the napkins. My daughters had been away from their friends for months. Their scripts certainly included the earliest possible exit to other more "happening" locations. My husband was thinking a lot of football. I don't think any of them had cleanup in their scripts, although there were some willing to meet the need. I set myself up for disappointment. My daughters, feeling my disappointment, were even more eager for an exit strategy.

The road rage, the scripting, the regret, the lack of focus and perspective—brokenhearted—it's all about me. "Jesus, heal my heart so that I can focus on You and perceive my circumstances from a higher and higher place, from Your perspective." Maturity is not about perfection.

It is the willingness to receive Jesus' healing as I embrace a process of focusing less and less on myself and more and more on God—a process of climbing higher and higher in the hot air balloon of God's perspective.

What is the latest script you have written?

Who were the participants? How did they do?

Were you disappointed?

How did Job get there—to focus and perspective? James brings our attention to Job, "We count those blessed who endured. You have heard of the endurance of Job and have seen the outcome of the Lord's dealings, that the Lord is full of compassion and is merciful."[7] In some versions, the word *endurance* is translated *patience*. When I read the book of Job, patience is not a word I would use to describe Job. I think patience implies a passive waiting. Job was certainly not passive. But that Greek word is also translated as *perseverance*. Job perservered—he was relentless in his pursuit of God! He pursued God's voice with every emotion, with every word. He wanted to hear what God had to say, but he wasn't ready to listen. He needed to verbalize his own thoughts, emotion, and frustration first. His nose was right up against that miserable, brick wall. Until Job uncovered all of his pain—physical, emotional, and spiritual—God's compassion and mercy seemed nonexistent and unattainable.

What about you? Are there times when your pain or your anger or your hurt seem all consuming? When your heart is broken, your nose is pushing against those rough bricks of the corner. It feels like even the atmosphere and the dirt are all about you!

You must remember that it's never all about you. **God would never be so inefficient as to make anything just all about you.** He will *always* use your circumstances to accomplish His purposes in you and for others, too.

God
would never be so in-
efficient
as to make
anything just
all about me!

The apostle Paul certainly exemplifies that concept. He was imprisoned in Rome—unjustly so. You can be sure that he wanted and prayed for God to release him so that he could visit and encourage the churches he had planted as well as to plant new churches.[8] Paul had so much that he wanted to accomplish for the King and the Kingdom. This time, it was not to be. However, while he was in Rome, he wrote wonderful letters: Ephesians, Philippians, Colossians, Philemon. I have read, reread, and been encouraged by these letters. Paul's inspired words have had a profound impact on my life. What if Paul's imprisonment was about me or you? Someone he never even knew would exist? Someone who would need the words he had written about two thousand years earlier?

Do you think Paul, in his difficult circumstances that were not of his own making, was regretting the past?[9]

Paul was living IN
the Present Moment
not FOR the
Present Moment.

Could he have been building up unreal expectations or scripting the future? Was he asking God where that abundant life was He had promised? So often when we are in the middle of difficulty, we read or think of the promise of Jesus, "I have come that they may have life and that they have it more abundantly" (John 10:10). Ahh—the Abundant

Life. But things are terrible, out of control, my heart is broken, my peace is gone, there is no joy. "Oh God, where is the peace and joy of the abundant life that You promised?"

Here's the problem: when my heart is broken, my mind is usually either in the past or the future. Have you ever driven somewhere, arrived safely at your destination, and realized that you didn't remember stopping at the stop sign? Or turning at the light? Where were you? Your heart and mind were either in the past or the future. Your drive was in the present, and you missed it. The present moment is one place you just can't seem to stay when your heart is broken.

Abundance is not the absence of pain, but the presence of God Almighty with you in your present circumstances.

The Abundant Life—in the Present Moment!
Divine Appointments, Revelation,
Holy Spirit Guidance—
All with Him in the Present Moment!

3   *Feel*

As you read the words in red, the words of Jesus in your Bible, or the prophetic Scriptures from the Old Testament, do you ever think about the emotion that's expressed? "He is despised and rejected by men, a Man of sorrows and acquainted with grief. And we hid, as it were, our faces from Him; He was despised, and we did not esteem Him." Stop here and go to your Bible to continue this passage from Isaiah 53:3–5. Read it out loud and hear the emotion in those verses: *despised, rejected, sorrow, grief, stricken, wounded.* Allow yourself to feel those emotions—some of them are probably very familiar.

What about Psalm 22:1? *Abandoned, rejected, isolated.* "My God, My God, why have You forsaken Me? Why are You so far from helping Me, and from the words of My groaning?" Look up this Psalm and read verses 6 through 8, verse 14, and verses 16 through 18. Do you feel the *shame, ridicule, humiliation,* and *depression? Do you feel the broken-heartedness* and *hopelessness?*

In Psalm 69:19–20, Jesus, through the pen of the psalmist, expresses more *shame* and *humiliation.* Then He laments, "Reproach has broken my heart, and I am full of heaviness . . . " His search for comfort was futile.

Feel Jesus' *anger* when He drives the money changers from the Temple,[1] and when He calls the Pharisees snakes[2] and white-washed tombs.[3] Feel His great sadness when Lazarus died,[4] and His *longing* to see Jerusalem accept Him.[5] Feel His *frustration* when He reprimands Peter.[6]

?

> If I had said the words Jesus said,
> what would I be feeling?

After the Last Supper, Jesus, beginning to convey His grief, walked to the Garden of Gethsemane. In the garden He expressed extreme emotion, verbally and physically. Not wanting to be alone in His distress, He had taken all of the disciples with Him to the Garden. When He proceeded even further into the depths of the garden, He pulled Peter, James, and John, His three closest friends, along with Him. His distress became more obvious and visible. "He said to them, 'My soul is exceedingly sorrowful, even to death. Stay here and watch with Me'" (Matthew 26:38).

Jesus had no wrong, erroneous, or faulty beliefs. He believed what was true—absolute Truth. **He *knew* the end from the beginning!** He knew that soon He would be sitting at the right hand of His Father, but He *felt* forsaken and abandoned by God.

> Jesus experienced the full range of emotion appropriately.

As a man, Jesus possessed the full range of God-given emotion to feel and to express. He experienced every emotion—appropriately. He *felt* those emotions He expressed in the garden fully, but He still said, "Not My will, but Yours" (Matthew 26:39). His action was not directed or determined by His emotion, yet His emotion was valid—adequately and appropriately expressed. Jesus can understand how we feel because *He has felt every emotion we feel.* Doesn't that make it perfect

and extremely comforting that He is our High Priest, forever interced
ing for us? (See Hebrews 4:14–16.)

Of course, I know there is a huge difference between Jesus and His
emotions, and me and my emotions. All of the emotions Jesus felt and
expressed were the result of true events, true circumstances, true actions or non-actions, and true motives of people who affected Him and
those He loved. I have a lot of emotions that are generated that same
way—based on truth. However, a lot of my emotions, many of those filling my glass, are based on false information, perceived circumstances,
false assumption of motive—*lies*.

As a child, I was always interpreting words, actions, and events, and
most of the time interpreting incorrectly. After all, I never had all the information. (Actually, none of us ever really has all of the information—
a good thing to remember.) Consequently, Satan had ample
opportunity to introduce life-altering lies. When Satan introduced a lie
such as "I must be unimportant, worthless," early in my life, then future
interpretation of my most disappointing interactions and circumstances triggered the emotions associated with that lie, allowing the lie
to become increasingly established in my being. It wasn't true, but I believed it.

When I came to a personal relationship with Jesus, accepting His payment for my debt of sin, I had a new awareness of my value to God, my
Father. However, because I was unaware of the origination point of the
lies, I would revert to those worthless-related emotions when those trig-
gering circumstances occurred. Satan had me exactly where he wanted
me—believing the opposite of what God said.

I was fully aware of who I was in Christ, who God created me to be—
chosen, valuable, His treasure—but my emotions just didn't consistently line up with that Truth. I was being robbed!

?

> In those times when your emotions don't match truth,
> what are your emotions telling you about what you believe?
>
> What is the lie that is replacing the truth?

Have you noticed that it is usually easier to believe the negative instead of the positive, the lie instead of the truth? Your mom buys you a new sweater. She says it looks great on you—brings out the color of your eyes. Your good friend says it looks good. Another girl makes a positive comment about it. Your teacher smiles and nods; you know she likes it. Then some "jerk" makes a snide comment about what the color of your sweater reminds him of—not a pretty picture. That sweater never comes out of the closet again; and you have a sudden, on-going self-consciousness of your eye color.

Something happens to me. I feel worthless, ugly, like a failure. I assume I shouldn't feel the way I feel. Did I somehow choose the emotion? I mistakenly think that my "feel bad" emotion must be a character flaw. Can I will myself out of it? I can't. I've tried, but I can't. **Emotion is not right or wrong—it just is.** Of course, there is more to it than that, but we'll get there as we continue.

?

> Do you feel wrong when you have negative emotions?
>
> What emotions make you feel wrong?

?

Do you feel right when you have positive emotions?

What emotions make you feel right?

Looking at Jesus and His emotion helps me know that emotion, even feel-bad emotion, is not ungodly, but God-given. I am fearfully and wonderfully made in the image of God, Jesus, and the Holy Spirit.[7] I was created to respond to my life experiences with emotion.

David, a prolific composer of heartfelt lyrics to God, filled each of those songs with emotion. Feeling anything more strongly than David would be difficult: *anger, depression, rejection, loneliness, joy, trust, security, gratitude, exultation.* God said that David—emotional David—was "a man after My own heart, who will do all My will" (Acts 13:22).

When I struggle to identify my emotion—I just don't know how I feel— I can read the Psalms and find one of David's emotional expressions that closely matches my feelings. I think sometimes we read some of the psalms and think we are getting a peek into David's private heart- cry to God. We forget that David wrote these words down, probably wrote the melodies, and then passed them out to the singers and musicians to be memorized for their next public worship time. David—authority, leader, and king—was not self-conscious or embarrassed by his feelings. (Would your journal make a good hymnal?)

In Psalm 31, David bursts with emotional pain: God, help me; my life is falling apart—the "I'm falling apart" kind of pain. "Have mercy on me, O Lord, for I am in trouble; my eye wastes away with grief, yes, my soul and my body! For my life is spent with grief, and my years with sighing; my strength fails because of my iniquity, and my bones waste away." [8]

Then David expresses the "everybody hates me; nobody loves me" kind of pain. "I . . . am repulsive to my acquaintances . . . I am forgotten like a dead man, out of mind; I am like a broken vessel . . . Fear is on every side . . . they scheme to take my life." [9]

Then, suddenly, David breaks out with, "But as for me, I trust in You, O Lord; I say, 'You are my God.'" He asks God to deliver him, to keep him from looking bad. "Do not let me be ashamed . . ." In fact, make those wicked people look bad; " . . . let them be silent in the grave." [10]

The end of the psalm is a release of words of glorious praise, gratitude, and encouragement to all who hope in God. "Blessed be the Lord, for He has shown me His marvelous kindness in a strong city! For I said in my haste, 'I am cut off from before Your eyes;' nevertheless You heard the voice of my supplications when I cried out to You. Oh, love the Lord, all you His saints! For the Lord preserves the faithful, and fully repays the proud person. Be of good courage, and He shall strengthen your heart, all you who hope in the Lord." [11]

You can read that entire psalm in less than two minutes. You may assume that's how long it took David to write it. He may have written it during the time he was hiding from Saul. He may have had some rough days, written a line or two at a time in a cave by the light of a candle. Whatever his struggle, he honestly expressed his emotions to God. Then one day, he saw or felt God's hand of protection and deliverance and began to write to reassure himself of his trust in God and to express his gratitude for God's unfailing faithfulness.

You may be able to identify with, even participate in David's anger, fear, or depression. But then, when you read the trust and praise part, you feel guilty for not being at that place. Just remember, David did not write it as fast as you can read it. We don't know how long it took him to process his emotion and move to trust and praise—the truth of God's love, protection, and provision.

?

How do you currently process emotion?

Do you ignore it?

Do you talk about it over and over again?

Do you go shopping?

Do you stew over it?

Jesus and David both modeled for us honest emotional expression. What better models could there be? Their emotion did not diminish their relationship with God. Their expression of emotion enhanced that precious relationship. An emotionless relationship is not really a relationship. **There is no place for intimacy void of emotion**.

David was not just venting. He was looking at each emotion, feeling and expressing it appropriately to God. Then, as a result of that honest expression, he was able to process emotionally the truth of who God is, and who he was—David was God's man. David's emotional response to that awareness was praise, awe of God's majesty and creation, joy, comfort, and contentment.

> David expressed his emotion appropriately to God—he wasn't just venting!

In Psalm 18, David asserts that God's deliverance is there for him "because He *delights* in me."[12] Regardless of David's mistakes, his anger, his fear, his depression—and the descriptive, unbridled expression of those emotions—David knows that he is valuable to God. God truly delights in him. The relationship that David had with God was always safe.

My time with my granddaughter, Margaret, is precious. Once I was visiting with her on a week of vacation. She was about eighteen months old at the time. I was staying with her one evening while her parents enjoyed a rare dinner alone. She was running around me, laughing, giggling. We were enjoying ourselves and each other. She ran into another room, and then came back, running past me again. I couldn't help but notice a new odor as she ran by. I looked at her little rear end and saw the tell-tale sag—she had filled her pants. I reined her in; her legs were still running as I lifted them from the floor. I got the mat, the box of wipes, and a plastic bag. She was not pleased with this break in our game. I held her down on the mat and began my task. This was a multiple wipe job—the mess was everywhere! I kept talking to her, making faces, anything to keep her relatively still. She was my joy, my delight. She was covered in a mess of her own making; she could never have cleaned herself. If she had not yielded to my hand, the mess would only have gotten messier. But, all during this "messy" process, I delighted in her! What she was covered in did not change who she was—my beloved granddaughter.

> No action or feeling will alter God's delight in me. His love for me is unconditional!

If I could only grasp His unconditional love. If I could only comprehend that there is no mess I can make, no emotion I can feel that will alter God's delight in me. His love for *me* is unconditional—that's what Jesus and David knew!

?

Is it possible for God to delight in me without
delighting in my behavior?

Can I believe that God delights in me even
when I have messed up?

Do I really believe God loves me unconditionally?

What keeps me from knowing and feeling
God's love consistently?

What do I think I would have to change for Him
to love me more?

**I can't do enough for Him to love me more.
There is no more!
I can't do bad enough for Him to love me less.
I am loved to the Max, Unending,
Unparalleled!**

4 Strategize

Satan had a lot of opportunities to introduce lies to my mind. My mother was always very guarded against pride. Now that's a very good thing, but her methods of conveying that to me as a child left a lot to be desired. She was always pointing out my mistakes and hesitated to affirm me. The lie that I came to believe was that I could never "do anything good enough" or "be good enough." When I accepted Jesus as my Savior, I grew in Him, and I learned more and more of God's Word, the Truth. However, those lies were still stuck in my mind and always kicked in at the worst possible times.

Some childhood messages are especially deceitful and subtle: a dad reassuring a child after that child has poorly executed some skill, then screaming or blasting someone on television who falls short of the mark in a similar skill; a mom questioning everything a child eats and commenting on the size of the new clothing that must be purchased. Some messages aren't subtle at all: "You're an idiot," or "You'll never amount to anything."

What are some of the messages that were conveyed to you in your childhood?

How have these messages affected you?

For me, the emotions resulting from these messages, as well as those subsequent circumstances that didn't go my way, typically had no place for expression. They were stuffed or denied. Of course, my parents stuffed and denied their emotions, too. If I began to express "negative" emotion, I was sent to my room. Since I was not allowed to "cry out" to my parents, **how could I learn that crying out to God was not only acceptable, it was imperative?** How could I know that He *wants* me to cry out to Him?

So maybe you have unresolved emotions in your vessel. You perhaps have not learned to appropriately express those emotions so they just keep piling up. *When something happens that stirs you up, you are in emotional pain.* No one likes pain. Over the years you have probably developed some methods of self-comfort—some ways to avoid or post-pone the pain. You wanted to achieve a "feel good" level at least equal to the "pain" level that you wanted to avoid or forget.

Obviously, different personality types may develop various patterns of self-comfort. If you have a melancholy personality, you may isolate and translate every pain into self-depreciation or depression. You may be the type of person who vents repeatedly to everyone, blaming and accusing others, not taking responsibility for your own emotions. You may just focus on something else: shopping, food, movies, books, sports. These activities may be healthy when you are not using them to avoid the pain. God may have just given you some R&R time, to refresh and renew, and a little time off from the pain, which is fine. However, if there are long-term consequences from these behaviors, you are using them inappropriately. Behaviors that are illegal and immoral—illicit sex or alcohol abuse or drug misuse—are always destructive and inexcusable.

My husband, Charlie, developed an acronym: *TRASH*. Trash behaviors are *Trends or Repeated Actions that Sabotage Healing*—short-term relief with long-term consequences. As previously stated, illegal or immoral behaviors are always wrong, but any "feel good" behaviors can also be destructive if they are used to avoid or mask the unwanted emotion.

In Genesis 4, we learn about Cain and Abel and some sacrifices.[1] These brothers had the offering of sacrifices modeled to them. Cain brought an offering of the fruit of the ground. It must have been wheat or corn or peaches or tomatoes. He maybe thought, "This is my best—the first of the crop, the biggest, the prettiest—of what I have grown." Abel brought the firstborn of his flock.

I believe that since blood sacrifice and its atoning provision is woven throughout Scripture, Cain and Abel knew what was required of them. Whether or not this is true, we do know that Cain was well aware of God's displeasure with him and His pleasure with Abel. Maybe Cain rationalized that since his crop was as good or as important as Abel's flock, his sacrifice should have been acceptable. He may have blamed Abel for his feelings of rejection, or perhaps he was just jealous or convicted of his own disobedience. A rationalizer is often a blamer. We know, though, that Cain was angry, and that he looked angry.[2]

Can you imagine God Himself asking you, "What's the matter?" We can be sure that God was not looking for information—Cain was the one that needed information. He needed to know why he was really angry. He could have even asked God, "What was wrong with my sacrifice? Don't You like me?"

Cain must not have wanted to talk about it with God because we have no record of any verbal response at all. What an opportunity—open dialogue with God![3] But Cain couldn't bring himself to face God or the truth.

God gives us, as He gave Cain, an opportune moment to shift directions—to make a choice for right behavior even though our emotions are in turmoil. He always gives us a window of opportunity to look at our pain and emotion with Him, and then to make a choice about our behavior. When we ignore that opportunity, the correct choice gets more and more difficult to make; and our behavior becomes more likely to act out our emotion. God wants us to verbalize the emotion so that we can act on truth. We want solid, deep roots—not like a reed that blows with every wind or even a breeze of circumstance or error in judgment or behavior. We want to be able to make a choice about how we respond to circumstances and people.

God told Cain that if he did not make the right choice, "Sin lies at the door. And its desire is for you, but you should rule over it."[4] I will either rule over sin, or it will rule over me. If I keep going in the wrong direction, not only does it get more and more difficult to change directions, at some point I have gone through the door where sin's rule begins. My chooser is virtually inoperative.

?

Look at the patterns of behavior that are your responses to difficult people or circumstances.

Where do you lose your choice not to sin?

Is your sin destructive words of anger or bitterness?

Is your sin a choice to engage in illegal or immoral activity?

How do you respond to difficult people or circumstances?

Cathy, the cartoon character, says, "I'll take a drive, but I won't go by the grocery. I'll go by the grocery, but I won't go in. I'll go in the grocery, but

I won't go down the candy aisle. I'll go down the candy aisle, but I won't pick up any candy. I'll pick it up, but I won't buy the candy. I'll buy the candy, but I won't eat it." The next frame shows little candy wrappers everywhere. Where was Cathy's door?

Mary Jo realized that she had an anger problem. Every Sunday afternoon her ex-husband came to pick up their daughter. He always pulled his big SUV into her yard, leaving ruts and mud. Toward the end of every week, Mary Jo's anger began to surface just anticipating those ruts. By Sunday, the anger was full-blown, destroying any opportunity to have a relationship with her ex that would benefit their daughter. For Mary Jo, the door was the car in the yard.

Mary Jo's HOPE group suggested a strategy to avoid that door—buying a concrete bench and putting it in the yard at the edge of the drive to block the SUV. One person vehemently argued against that action, stating that it was the guy's problem, not Mary Jo's. But, it was Mary Jo's anger that was causing her stress, robbing her of peace, and leading to sinful and caustic words and actions.

Mary Jo actually bought that bench for her yard. She reported a much improved week, more peace, and over time, amicable communication with her ex-husband. (Think of how much less emotion the daughter received in her emotional vessel as a result of that bench—a small price to pay for a huge emotional payoff.)

Joe is a great guy, but unknown to most, is a sex addict. When he fights or even disagrees with his wife, he disappears from the room to avoid the conflict and confrontation. He heads for the den, sits down, and picks up the remote control. After only a few minutes of surfing cable TV, he comes across some lingerie models. This triggers his addiction, and within a short time he is in front of his computer downloading porn off the internet. Where is his door? What strategy could he use to avoid it?

When I present this example in a HOPE Workshop, I get several suggestions: disconnect cable, don't sit in front of the TV, don't pick up the remote. If Joe doesn't have a strategy, he is monster bait—that monster is sin waiting at the door!

> Where is your door?
>
> When are you vulnerable?

We read in 1 Kings 18 and 19 about an incredible event. Elijah challenged 450 prophets of Baal and 400 prophets of Asherah to a sacrifice duel designed to identify, once and for all, the one true God. The bull chosen by the false prophets was prepared and placed on an altar. Everything was there and ready, except the fire. The 950 false prophets went first. They cried out to Baal for fire. They jumped around; they screamed. They cut themselves—still no fire. I would imagine that 950 weird people could make a lot of noise, and it went on for more than twelve hours![5]

Then, just before dark, Elijah said it was his turn.[6] He repaired a broken-down altar, dug a trench around it, and laid the wood and the sections of bull on the altar. He called for pots of water over and over. When the poured out water had drenched the bull, the wood, the stones, and completely filled the trench, Elijah calmly prayed to God. "Hear me, O Lord, hear me, that this people may know that You are the Lord God, and that You have turned their hearts back to You again."[7]

Immediately, the "fire of the Lord" fell on the sacrifice.[8] It was all *consumed*—the bull, the wood, the stones, the dust, and all the water in the trench. What a God show! All the people watching fell on their faces and cried, "The Lord, He is God!" Imagine how Elijah must have felt: *relief, awe, I-told-you-so jubilation and vindication.*

Elijah couldn't stay in that thrill of victory too long—he had another project that was also at the climax point. He had been praying for rain to end a very long drought and just *knew* that it was about to happen. He even told the king that there was about to be a downpour. He prayed and asked his servant to go look toward the sea for a sign of rain—nothing. Again and again, six more times, he sent his servant to look. The seventh time, the servant reported a small cloud. Elijah stood up; the rain was coming![9]

As Elijah began to run for cover, he was given a chilling message from the queen, Jezebel, that he would be dead at her command within twenty-four hours. Then he was running, not just from the rain, but for his life. Elijah had suddenly plunged to the agony of defeat. In despair he collapsed, exhausted physically, emotionally, and spiritually. Elijah prayed to die, and then he fell asleep.[10]

An angel serving food woke Elijah to eat. He ate and fell back asleep. The angel woke him up again to eat. The story continues, but what we see here is that God knew that Elijah was tired, hungry, and experiencing a huge emotional let-down following a spiritual high—three of the most vulnerable times for approaching the door where sin is waiting. I suspect that he was also angry and lonely. He even told God that he was the only prophet left.[11] (Emotional pain can be so isolating.)

The acronym *HALTS* describes those vulnerable times: *Hungry, Angry, Lonely, Tired, Successful.* When you are two of the five, beware! Eat, rest, talk to God and a safe person.

Ask God to help you identify the following:
- What events precede your failures?
- What pushes your buttons?

- Is there a time of day, day of the week, or certain location? Are there surroundings, specific situations, or the same people involved?
- Do you experience extreme lows after a major high, following any type of success including a spiritual success?

A good strategy is two-pronged: not just a "Do Not" strategy, but also a "Do" strategy.

Know what/who they are and plan your strategy! A good strategy is two-pronged: not just a "Do Not" strategy, but also a "Do" strategy. I am not going to sit down in front of the TV; I am going to take a walk and pray. I am not going to buy candy; I am going to buy nuts. Don't be at the mercy of your circumstances. Know where your door is and stay away from it!

?

What strategy have you used to avoid TRASH behaviors?

How consistently has it worked?

If you have had inconsistent results, stop and pray— ask God for a new strategy.

My new "Do Not" strategy:

My new "Do" strategy:

5   Relate

Heads up! Here it comes! The big, red emotional ball—somebody threw it at me. I can feel heat starting to creep up my body. I feel my neck and shoulders start to stiffen. Emotion is quickly developing.

All of us have certain people or specific topics that push our buttons—the things that always upset us. This often happens in conversation, maybe with a family member, a boss, a co-worker, or whoever triggers something negative from the past, a political topic, or anything that puts you in a defensive position. Let's think of each of those "button-pushing" situations as an "emotional ball-throwing" experience.

When my dad (now gone to be with the Lord) was a widower and living alone, he would call me and say in a whiney voice, "I'm all alone." Now the words were true, but I had known my dad a long time and could pretty accurately interpret the meaning of his words. I knew that he meant more than he was saying. So my brain, without any conscious effort on my part, made an immediate translation. The words I heard were not, "I'm all alone," but "You haven't been over to visit me in a long time. When are you coming?"

Have you ever heard people say, "I know what she's really saying," or "I know what he really means." Their brains are making that translation from what is actually spoken to what they assume is meant. *Assumption*—it will get us in trouble every time. Ultimately, it will not matter in a ball-throwing situation if the assumption is correct or not. Those assumptions are judgments of another person's heart or motives. Jesus admonished us not to judge; if we do, we will be judged.[1]

When I made that assumption, translated it in my head, and heard what I believed my dad was *really* saying, I was catching the ball. If I caught it, I would throw it back. To throw the ball back meant that my *verbal response* to the thrower (my dad) addressed what I heard ("You haven't been over to visit in a long time"), not the actual words that were spoken ("I'm all alone"). So I said to my dad words of defense. "I have good reasons for not coming to see you. I've had responsibilities, meetings, errands, and other things."

Guess what my dad was going to do? I had judged, and he would judge, too. His brain took my excuses, my defensiveness, and translated my words. He heard, "I care about everything, anything, more than I care about you, Dad." He caught the ball. It was a bigger ball this time because each time that ball went back and forth, the emotional level increased.

By the time our conversation was over, and I hung up the phone, I was angry; and his feelings were hurt. I felt that he wasn't interested in anything I was doing. The message he heard was that I didn't care about him. Can you believe it? All of those emotions, emotions that would affect the rest of my day and set me up for the next ball-throwing incident, were based on *words that no one said!*

Sue, a middle-aged woman, was going to assume caregiving responsibility for her mother while her brother and sister-in-law, the primary caregivers, were on vacation. Sue and her mother had always had a very strained relationship, but Sue, like most of us, never outgrew the desire for her mother's approval and affirmation. As the time for her responsibility approached, Sue started trying to think of things she and her mother could do together that would please her mother. (She did a lot of script writing—remember script writing in Chapter 2?) She had one idea that seemed especially promising. Her mother would really appreciate this one!

On her way to her own doctor's appointment, Sue called her mom. "Mom, I've got a great idea for next week! I'll take you to Atlanta to see Aunt Ann. We'll go out for lunch, and maybe do a little shopping. It will give you a chance to see Aunt Ann—we'll have a really good time."

Her mother's immediate response was, "Why would I want to do a thing like that?" Her tone of voice was very confrontative and antagonistic. Those words pierced Sue's heart like a dagger, and her blood pressure soared. The big red ball hit hard. This was a repeat of years of previous conversations. Sue's brain made the instant translation, and she heard, "Why would I want to go anywhere or do anything with you? You have crummy ideas. I don't even like you."

How can we learn to dodge that ball? We don't have to catch it. What does that look like? High percentages of conversations in our culture are based on assumption. We are generally terrible at communication. We automatically assume so much when someone speaks to us. Catching the ball and throwing it back is a habit. It takes time and effort—and God's help—to break the old habits and develop new communication patterns, not based on assumption, but on actual words that are spoken.

How can I get my brain to stop that instant translation? I just want to respond to the words, not the tone of voice, not the body language, not all the relationship history. When listening to my dad, I decided the best method for me was to imagine that those words were being spoken by a "little old lady" in the grocery store check-out line. I didn't know her; I'd probably never see her again. I wanted to help her maintain peace—which, by the way, helped me maintain my own peace.

My dad's words were, "I'm all alone." If the "little old lady" had said those words to me, how would I have responded? I would say, "I'm sorry you are feeling lonely today." Or, maybe just, "I'm sorry." So, if I responded with those words to my dad, and he really wanted to tell me that he thought I should come over to see him, hopefully, he would say so. But, either way, I've validated him—I heard him. I heard his emotion. If I was convicted that I needed to see him soon—*not guilted*, but convicted—I might also have told him when I was coming to see him. Dodging that ball could force much improved communication and ultimately an improved relationship.

Sue could have answered her mom, "I'm sorry that you don't want to go. I'd like to see Aunt Ann, and I think I'll go at a later time. If you change your mind, just let me know, and we'll go together." Then she could have just gone to a different topic—a safe topic.

?

Who pushes your buttons? Throws the ball at you?

How can you dodge the ball?

Another interesting aspect of ball-throwing is emotional responsibility. If I catch the ball my dad throws, he feels justified in holding me responsible for his emotions. From his perspective, it's up to me to make him feel better. If I take that responsibility, if I catch the ball—it is up to me to make him feel better. Maybe my response to catching the ball is to feel so guilty that I drop what I'm doing and head over there to make him feel better. Over time, as this happens again and again, I will feel resentful about what I perceive to be manipulation, and will feel that I am being held hostage emotionally.

Taking emotional responsibility for other people sabotages relationship and communication. If I respond out of guilt and feel that I am responsible to change my dad's emotions, my communication and relationship with him will not really improve. If I respond in anger or withdrawal, there will be hurt feelings.

Individual personalities respond differently—I may have a different response when I catch the ball than you do when you catch it. However, responding out of guilt, anger, or hurt never promotes genuine communication or intimacy in relationship.

Remember that ball throwers and ball catchers both have emotional vessels that are very full of unresolved emotion, possibly overflowing. You never know what is in someone else's vessel. (You probably don't know what is in your own.) Whatever is coming at you is a conglomeration of all the emotion in the ball thrower's vessel. Don't even try to figure it out in the context of the moment.

List possible ball-dodging responses to the following:

"I can't talk now."
You hear, "I don't want to talk to you."

"Can't you find your paper?"
You hear, "You can't keep up with anything."

"Is that what you're wearing to dinner?"
You hear, "That outfit is tacky—it makes you look fat."

Some days I may think I am doing really well spiritually, mentally, and emotionally; and then something happens. Somebody does something or says something, or maybe something bad just happens. And, I react—I catch the ball!

Ball throwers and ball catchers both have emotional vessels that are overflowing.

What gave me the propensity to catch those balls anyway? When and how did I get all those buttons? Most of the time, the buttons were set by loss experiences and from the lies I believed that were introduced in those events: *I'm worthless. I can't ever do anything right. I will never be good enough. He doesn't/won't/can't love me anymore. I'm a mistake. Something bad is going to happen. If I don't do it right, I am worthless/unlovable.*

The person who said those words or performed the action that pushed my button was probably unaware that the ball had been thrown—even if that person was the very one who was involved in setting my button in the first place. While that does not excuse their confrontative or accusing behavior, I am responsible for the way I respond.

So what lies did I hear and respond to yet again when my dad said, "I'm all alone." Remember, I translated it to, "You haven't been over to visit in a long time." But the lies—my buttons—were *if I don't do it right, I am worthless. I can never please my dad. I should have done more. I should be better. He never cares about me.*

I jumped to the defense mode when I assumed that my dad was thinking that I was worthless or lazy or irresponsible. When I caught the ball, I just further solidified those lies in my being. My assumption and resulting defensiveness hurt **me.** I resorted to comfort patterns, TRASH behaviors (Trends, Repeated Actions Sabotaging Healing—Chapter 4). The belief of one lie led to bizarre thinking—regretting the past and fantasizing about the future, faulty thinking about where I was, and what people were going to think or do. Satan had a hey-day with my place of vulnerability!

When interactions are consistently failed dodge ball matches, you must not only develop the habit of dodging the ball, you must also identify your buttons and cooperate with God in the process of mind renewal. When you are successful at dodging the ball, let the emotions that surface serve the purpose that God intended. He will show you the areas where you have unresolved emotions and help you identify the lies that are affecting you. *Only mind renewal will transform brain translation.*

Let's look at the big picture. Think of God opening up a tent—*the* tent—of glory when Jesus was resurrected. Oh, what a tent—the glory of righteousness— the blinding light of glory. The body and blood of Jesus is the fabric, support, substance, and essence of the tent, and all it covers. Look at where we are—covered by His righteousness! Look at whose we are—we are His, bought with a price! What happens when shame, fear, perfectionism, and worthlessness take control of our thoughts, emotions, and even our actions?

> Dodge the balls.
> Identify your buttons.
> Cooperate with God in the process of renewing your mind.

Hebrews 2:11 tells us that Jesus (who sanctifies us), *and* all of us who are accepting of His payment for our sin and have given ourselves to Him (we who are being sanctified)—the tent *and* all of us who have stepped under the tent—are all one unit. A single unit of glory!

Satan does not have the power to pull us from that tent. So, how does he get to us? He sabotages our thinking. I'm in the tent. I'm basking in His glory. I'm in Jesus, but sadly and deceptively I'm thinking, "Look at me. I have these black spots of sin. Everyone sees my spots. I don't deserve to be here. I'm probably going to be kicked out"—*shame.*

Or *fear*—"What if none of these people want me here? I can't let anyone see who I really am. I need to keep my secrets." Or *worthlessness*—

"I don't/can't qualify for this. I don't deserve to be here. If they really knew me, they wouldn't like me, wouldn't want me here, wouldn't think I belong here."

> Where is your most obvious point of vulnerability to the enemy?
>
> Shame?
>
> Fear?
>
> Worthlessness?
>
> What lies have you believed that keep you stuck?

Then there are those of us who keep trying to prove to ourselves and to God that we are good enough to be in the tent—we can hold up our part. We can't let up, can't let down our guard. There's always more to do— more and more to do. *Perfectionism!* How exhausting! Gotta read enough, pray enough, say enough, do enough, be nice enough, serve enough—enough, enough. And, it's really only worthwhile if someone else in the tent notices. Perfectionists always notice if *someone else* under the tent isn't enough.

> Do you find yourself on the treadmill of not being good enough?
>
> Not doing enough?

?

How does being on the treadmill of perfectionism affect your ability to focus as well as your energy level?

Do you see the problem? Satan has succeeded in getting our focus off the *glory* of the tent. We are not looking at Jesus. Our gaze is fixed on ourselves and our weaknesses. The tent is about a unit, a oneness with Jesus. We diminish, minimize, lessen the significance of the glory in our own eyes when we are focused on our weaknesses or our strengths. The reality is that the blinding glory of the tent *overcomes* **all** darkness. There is so much to see in the glory, why would I want to waste my time and energy trying to spot darkness in myself or anyone else?

Wow—we all have some work to do! As you continue to read and work through this book, be honest about how you feel. Learn how to pour out your soul to God. As you pour out your soul honestly, authentically, and thoroughly, your feelings and emotions are released to His glory. When you deny, stuff, or hide your emotions, you quarantine those parts of your mind and heart and separate yourself from His glory, setting yourself up for Satan's lies.

But in the meantime, as you learn and experience this process, practice dodging the ball. Ask God to show you when the ball is coming. Sometimes you are in such a rut that you don't see any options to your responses. Talk through some of your dodge ball conversations with a trusted friend, or with someone who has had some success at dodging the ball. Develop a strategy. Remember, as you continue to work on your challenging relationships, God is the One who changes your heart and renews your mind.

6   *Lose and Gain*

There was some serious ball-throwing going on in Jacob's household. The family dynamic was in trouble from the beginning. Leah (Jacob's number 1 wife) gave her husband four sons, quickly out-producing Rachel (Jacob's number 2, yet favored and most dearly loved wife).[1] A frustrated Rachel gave her handmaiden, Bilhah, to Jacob. Bilhah produced two sons. In retaliation, Leah gave her handmaiden, Zilpah, to Jacob; and Zilpah had two sons for Jacob. Then Leah gave birth to two more sons and one daughter—a total of eleven children. Rachel, Jacob's beloved Rachel, was childless.

At last God heard Rachel's cry to Him, and she gave birth to a son, Joseph.[2] Can you imagine the joy in the household—at least a small segment of the household? The long-awaited child born of love. But, can you also imagine the competition and stress that would occur among four wives and twelve children when the footing was anything but equal?

A few years later Rachel died as she was giving birth to Joseph's brother, Benjamin. Benjamin was a favorite also, but Joseph had already captured Jacob's heart. Without their loving mother to care for them, Joseph and Benjamin were probably cared for by servants and the other three wives—jealous wives.

On one occasion after the Jacob family had settled in Canaan, Joseph, now seventeen, was helping four of his brothers with the flocks.[3] These brothers, the sons of Bilhah and Zilpah, must not have done it right, whatever "it" was, because Joseph hustled back to Dad and tattled on them. Jacob not only listened to Joseph, but he made his favorite son a beautiful, colorful coat. That coat was a visible symbol of what the other brothers knew all along—they would never achieve the love and attention that Joseph got. There was nothing that they could do to improve their standing with Dad. Their irritation and intolerance for Joseph progressed to hatred—everything they said to him was a put-down, a barb, an insult—words of hate.

Then Joseph had the nerve to tell them about his dream, and they hated him even more.[4] In Joseph's dream all the brothers were working together tying up sheaves—stalks of wheat. Joseph's sheaf stood tall, and the sheaves of the brothers bowed down to Joseph's sheaf.

Can you believe that after the negative response he received from telling that first dream, Joseph told his brothers about his second dream, too? In that dream the sun, moon, and stars (coincidentally, eleven stars) all bowed down to Joseph.[5] When his father heard this dream, he rebuked Joseph, asking him if he really thought his father, mother, and eleven brothers were all going to bow down to him. The rebuff Jacob had for Joseph did not keep the brother's hatred toward Joseph from growing even stronger.

Genesis 37:12–13 seems to imply that the brothers did the work, and Joseph attended his father (which might also have been work, but I doubt that the brothers saw it that way). Jacob asked Joseph to go check on his brothers and the flocks—just to see how they were doing—and bring back word of their welfare.

The brothers saw Joseph coming in the distance and recognized him—maybe it was the famous coat that gave him away.[6] "Here comes Dreamer Boy." They just wanted to kill him. After all, Joseph was the source of a lot of their grief. Reuben, the oldest, took responsibility and tried to soften their thirst for blood by suggesting that they just throw Joseph in a nearby pit.

When Joseph got to his brothers, they immediately stripped him of his beautiful coat and threw him down into the pit.[7] Can you just imagine

Joseph's horror and disbelief? How could this be happening? The brothers, with a sense of satisfactory vengeance in their hearts, sat down to eat dinner.

Content and eating, the brothers looked up to see dust on the horizon— a caravan of camels. It looked like a band of Ishmaelites heading toward Egypt to sell their goods.[8] Unfortunately for Joseph, Reuben had left the guys for some reason. In his absence, Judah suggested that instead of killing him, they just sell Joseph to the Ishmaelites.

What must Joseph have thought when they pulled him up out of the pit? Maybe relief—only to be overwhelmed with panic when he realized he had been sold to strangers. He had been sold by his brothers—his family—to strangers. It was all over! Life as he had known it was over. What about his father? Would he come to help him? Would no one come to his rescue?

When have you felt that life as you knew it was over?

Did you feel that no one would come to your rescue?

When that caravan of Ishmaelites arrived in Egypt, Joseph was sold to Potiphar, the captain of Pharaoh's guard.[9] Perhaps for as long as ten years, Joseph faithfully served Potiphar. From the beginning, while Joseph worked in Potiphar's house, God was with him. He did such a good job that it was noticeable—the work ethic, the integrity. Potiphar transferred more and more responsibility to Joseph until he was overseeing everything that Potiphar had. The more responsibility Joseph was given, the more God blessed Potiphar. Joseph surely must have felt content in his relationship with God as well as satisfaction with his productivity in Potiphar's business and household.

Through these years, Joseph matured from a teenager to a man, a very handsome and well-built guy.[10] This did not go unnoticed by Mrs. Potiphar. She flirted with Joseph shamelessly, bluntly asking for a physical relationship. Joseph tactfully replied that he would not betray Potiphar, or sin against God by doing such a thing. Mrs. Potiphar knew her power—she would win. She would get what she wanted, eventually.

But no—Joseph would not give in. He was determined to be his best for his master and his God. One day Mrs. Potiphar caught him alone and accosted him, grabbing his robe.[11] He turned and ran, losing his robe to her grasp. She screamed, accusing Joseph of very improper advances. When her husband returned, she recounted her fabricated story until Potiphar rose in anger to send Joseph to prison. (Obviously, Potiphar's trust in Joseph was not totally destroyed because a crime of that magnitude normally meant death to the perpetrator.)

Falsely accused, unjustly incarcerated, Joseph's reputation was ruined. His life over—again! At least initially, he wore fetters and irons—physically and emotionally painful.[12] He was alone—except God was with him. Once again God was merciful to Joseph and gave him favor with the prison keeper.[13] Eventually, the prison keeper handed the prison and all its residents over to Joseph's watchful eye. Whatever Joseph did, wherever Joseph was, God prospered him.

?

Is it difficult for you to recognize God's favor in adverse circumstances?

Back at the palace, Pharaoh had some frustration with his butler and baker. He went ballistic, and in a rage, threw them into Joseph's prison. Genesis 40:4 says that Joseph served them. I think if I had to be in jail, Joseph's jail would be the place to be.

One morning Joseph noticed that these two men under his charge were looking rather dejected.[14] Can you imagine that even with his personal history, Joseph was actually living in the present moment and observant enough to spot the demeanor of these two prisoners? Joseph, a man with a servant's heart, asked these men what was wrong. Why did they look so sad?

> Do you look for opportunities to serve others or consider their circumstances when you are hurting, or is it all about you?

Both men had experienced troubling dreams the night before, and neither man could come up with an interpretation. Joseph acknowledged that all interpretations belonged to God, and then requested that they tell him their dreams. His God would provide the interpretations. First, the butler recounted his dream, and Joseph gave a very encouraging interpretation: in three days, the butler would be out of jail and back on the job.

Joseph followed the interpretation with a request of his own. In hope of being released from prison, he asked that the butler kindly remember him, an innocent man who had been captured from his homeland, and mention him to Pharaoh.

The baker was excited about the interpretation of the butler's dream, and so proceeded to tell Joseph his dream. Joseph's interpretation was not only devastating, but also true. The very day that the butler was restored to his position, the baker was hanged.

Knowing that the butler would be back in good graces with Pharaoh, Joseph no doubt was anticipating that his prison experience would soon end. However, the butler in his relief and thrill of freedom and life, forgot Joseph. For two years he forgot Joseph. But then, Pharaoh himself had a dream and then a second dream—very disturbing and perplexing dreams.[15]

When everyone within Pharaoh's beck and call failed to interpret the dreams, the butler suddenly remembered Joseph, interpreter of dreams. Joseph, now thirty years old, was called, cleaned-up, shaved, dressed, and presented to Pharaoh. He quickly let Pharaoh know the interpretation was not his, but God's.

God clearly revealed to Joseph that Pharoah's dreams foretold the events of the next fourteen years in Egypt. Joseph emphasized to Pharaoh the two dreams firmly indicated that God would carry out this time in exactly the way the dreams indicated—seven years of great harvest and plenty followed by seven years of blight, depletion, and famine. God immediately gave Joseph an action plan, a strategy that would save Pharaoh's kingdom.

We know that Pharaoh chose Joseph as the right man—full of God's Spirit, to carry out the plan. But until the moment he was chosen, Joseph did not know where the mighty hand of God was taking him. He did know that he was out of prison and in front of Pharaoh. He had gone from the worst location to the best location, the grungiest to the cleanest. God had made a way! His brothers had not bowed down to him, but now everyone in Egypt except Pharaoh had. He had a new wife, a new reputation, a new job, a new calling, and a new robe—one of honor that would not be stripped away with lies and deceit as the other two coats had been (the coat torn from him by his brothers, and the coat grabbed and held by Mrs. Potiphar). It had been a long thirteen years away from his family, but now Joseph was calling all the shots. He saw God's vision for the land and promptly got to work.

Do you think this sudden propulsion into the role of hero made him forget the life he lost? During the first seven years as head honcho, Joseph and his wife had two sons: *Manasseh,* which means "for God has made me forget all my toil and all my father's house," and *Ephraim,* which means "for God has caused me to be fruitful in the land of my affliction."[16] These names sound to me as if Joseph was expressing an emotional mixture of sadness and thanksgiving. He was the victim and the victor.

The famine was not confined to Egypt. When Joseph's family in Canaan heard there was food in Egypt, all of Joseph's brothers—except Benjamin the beloved—headed for Egypt.[17] In Egypt, there was no buying grain by anyone without a face-to-face encounter with Joseph. Can you imagine Joseph's feelings when he saw his brothers in the line?

Joseph had stashed those relationships with his father and brothers in boxes which he placed neatly on a shelf in his heart—like putting shoe boxes on a closet shelf. When he saw his brothers, those boxes must have suddenly tumbled off, crashing on his head!

> What circumstances or relationships that you have already "dealt with" (for instance, someone you have previously forgiven) seem to sometimes surface?

When it was finally their turn, the brothers *bowed* low to the ground to Joseph. Don't you know that those teenage dreams vaulted from memory to the present moment in a flash? Aha! Now it was the brothers' turn to be desperate. Joseph's stuffed teenage emotions of rejection were probably screaming in his head, "I told you so!" Then the realization hit hard that life in Canaan had continued without him. Had his brothers changed? What kind of men had they turned out to be?

Instead of verbalizing all his questions and emotions, Joseph addressed his brothers harshly—careful not to reveal his identity.[18] He accused them of being spies and demanded to see the phantom younger brother. Then he threw them all in jail for three days. The raw pain of his youth was right in his face. He took advantage of his position to enjoy a measure of retaliation without giving himself away. He spent those three days processing some of that emotion. The ostracized, abused little brother walked into the big picture conclusion: *fear of God*. God's hand was, and always had been, on him!

On the third day, head honcho Joseph called the ten foreign men into his presence and proposed a deal for them based on his own present emotional reality. The deal: one of the ten would stay in the prison house, while the other nine returned to Canaan with all the food they needed. Then they must return to Egypt with the younger brother. Joseph determined that the brother in jail would serve as surety to guarantee the return and further interaction with his family.

Confronted with no other choice, the brothers agreed to the deal.[19] Realizing the gravity of their situation, the weight of guilt of the past surfaced, overwhelming them. In their own Hebrew language, the agonizing brothers argued about their guilt, and the distress they had witnessed in the young, terrified Joseph. Reuben battered them with the "you should have listened" statements of blame.

?

> Is your difficult circumstance and your pain the result
> of someone else's wrong choices?
>
> Do you take responsibility for your own wrong choices?
>
> Do you blame someone else for your wrong choices?

As Joseph eavesdropped on the rehash of his last moments with his family, the pain of those moments long ago overtook his heart. The tears began to surface, and the big man in charge had to quickly turn away to cry.

When he had recovered his composure, Joseph came back to his brothers, selected Simeon as the hostage and handcuffed him. Is it possible that Joseph selected Simeon because he was the second oldest after Reuben? Since Reuben was absent when it was decided to sell Joseph, perhaps Joseph held Simeon responsible for the actions of all the brothers. While Judah had been the one to suggest selling Joseph, that was at least a better alternative than killing him, which seemed to be the plan of the majority.

So with Simeon relegated to prison, Joseph made sure the brothers had the grain they needed; and directed that the money they had used for payment be slipped down into their sacks.[20] As the anxious brothers camped for the night on the way home to Canaan, one of the brothers discovered the money in his sack. The overwhelming guilt and fear flooded over them again. In horror, they determined that all of their current woeful circumstances were God's vengeance for their actions of over twenty years earlier.

Father Jacob could not believe the turn of events. No Joseph, no Simeon, and now they wanted to take Benjamin! Fate was against him.[21] He would not hear of it. No way were they taking Benjamin! Sorry about Simeon, but the risk was too great.

The brothers let it go until everyone was hungry again.[22] Jacob told them to just go back to Egypt and buy more food. But Jacob could not feel their terror at the thought of returning without honoring the conditions that Egypt's governor had set. Benjamin had to go, or they weren't going. After lots of second-guessing of the actions and words of the brothers, Jacob finally faced reality—they would all die without food. He sweetened the pot with presents, doubled the money that had somehow been returned, packed up Benjamin, and prayed for mercy. If he had to grieve, he would just grieve—no way around it. He had no choice.

When Joseph recognized the travelers standing meekly before him, his eyes searched out Benjamin. When his gaze fastened on Benjamin, a plan materialized. Joseph directed his servants to take the men to his home and to begin arranging a noontime feast. Fear gripped the brothers anew—what was happening? Was it the money they had found in their bags? Were they all destined to be slaves?

Upon arrival at Joseph's house, they began their defense to the steward, explaining what had happened and proclaiming their innocence.[23] The steward offered them peace, gave credit to God for giving them the money, and brought Simeon to them. Then, surprisingly, the steward gave them water, advised them of the upcoming meal, washed their feet, and even fed their donkeys. Maybe things were looking up.

When Joseph arrived at his home, assumedly for lunch, the brothers hurriedly presented to him the gifts sent by Jacob and—once again— *bowed* before him. Joseph asked about the well-being of their father; and when they responded, they *bowed* yet again. Then Joseph looked squarely at his brother Benjamin, the son of his own mother, and asked if this was the younger brother of whom they had spoken.

As Joseph spoke a blessing to Benjamin, the emotion rose in his heart and in his throat. Once again he had to make a quick exit to conceal his emotion.[24] He simply could not stop the tears. He cried in the privacy of his room until he was cried out. When the tears finally came to an end, he washed his face, and returned to his guests so that the meal could be served.

The brothers were astonished when they realized that they had been seated in their birth order. Joseph himself brought each of them servings of the food that had been set before him, giving obvious preference to Benjamin by serving him five times as much as the others. As they ate and drank—good food, good wine—they began to relax and enjoy the moment.

But, Joseph's processing wasn't complete. He was obviously still working through those emotions that had been hidden so deep for so long. He directed the steward to fill every brother's sack with as much as each man could physically carry, and to hide each man's grain money in his sack. He then commanded the steward to put the silver cup, probably the very one Joseph had used at lunch, in Benjamin's sack.[25]

Early the next morning, the brothers and their donkeys were loaded and sent on their way. When they were barely out of sight, Joseph sent his steward after them to accuse them of stealing from the governor. They couldn't believe it—they had even brought back extra money. They were, after all, men of integrity. They would never steal from the governor. The brothers were so confident in their trust in each other that they promised the steward that if any one of them had stolen the cup, he would die; and the rest of them would willingly become slaves. The steward began searching each one's sack, beginning with Reuben. Every sack was clean until he got to Benjamin's sack. There was the cup! The brothers were devastated! It was all over!

> **?**
>
> What circumstances have you experienced that appeared to be the END?
>
> An injustice?
>
> A death?
>
> A betrayal?
>
> A job loss?
>
> A personal failure?
>
> How did your perspective affect the outcome?

They headed back in shame and disbelief to Joseph's house, *falling on the ground* before him. Joseph accused them of stealing, and thinking he was an idiot. Judah, humbly accepting the situation, took charge of the reply. He had promised Jacob that he would be personally responsible for Benjamin. When Joseph suggested that Benjamin stay in Egypt as a slave and the rest of the brothers return home, Judah begged for mercy, attempting to convey the severity of the pain that Benjamin's absence would bring to their aging father. He emotionally expressed the immeasurable consequences and the devastation that the loss of Benjamin would bring to the household.

Joseph was overwhelmed with pain—Judah's pain, Jacob's pain, and his own pain. He ordered all his staff to leave, and he began to wail.[26] Joseph's guttural wails were so deep, so intense, that even those in Pharaoh's house could hear his pain. What pain! Pain held in his heart and in his body for so many years. What relief! Relief at seeing his brothers and the hope of seeing his father after so many years. What awareness! Awareness of his part in God's plan. *Pain, relief, anger, understanding,* all being loudly expressed.

Joseph beckoned his brothers to come close, and he finally disclosed his identity. He had spent the last several weeks and months processing so many emotions, and had come to the place where he knew for certain that all his pain was purposeful. It was never all about him; it wasn't even just about his family. God had made a way to preserve not only Joseph, his father, and his brothers, but thousands and thousands of lives; and He had used a horrible thing to do it. Joseph had lost relationships, freedom, home, culture, language, security, expectations, dreams, trust, identity—but oh, what he had gained. The process wasn't easy or fast. But, the wisdom, knowledge, and relationship with God were worth it all!

> God made
> a way!
> Not just for one,
> but for many.

?

If you attended a HOPE Workshop, how were you affected by seeing all of your losses on paper?

What *patterns* of loss and *patterns* of response do you see in your own life?

7 Hope

If only Jacob had not presented Joseph that fabulous, colorful coat! Maybe his brothers would not have resented him so much. They might have learned to love him over time. Maybe they wouldn't have sold him. Mrs. Potiphar wouldn't have lied about him; he wouldn't have endured those years in prison. True, he would not have realized the position of main man in Egypt, but wouldn't he have had a wonderful life in Canaan?

Joseph certainly had reason to resent his dad—Jacob's unabashed favoritism set Joseph up for a failed relationship with his brothers. He also had a good excuse to be bitter toward his brothers, hold on to the injustice of the Potiphars, and begrudge the short-term memory of the butler. Joseph was definitely a victim of unreal expectations, jealousy, hatred, injustice, and bigotry. In the only record we have of Joseph's view of his victimization, he told the butler and the baker what happened to him—how he came to be in a prison in Egypt—without blaming or slandering anyone.[1] He didn't blame his circumstances on his father, his brothers, or the Potiphars.

Joseph always seemed to surface with the "when life gives you lemons, make lemonade" philosophy. That seems so unrealistic, doesn't it? How did Joseph, the perpetual victim, get that perspective?

Human, worldly perspective is about TIME—my time—what I can see, what I can hear, what I can touch, what I can smell, and what I can taste. All of that is overlaid with how I feel, or might feel, or did feel about what happened at the time. Joseph somehow moved beyond his senses, beyond his 24/7 life to a timeless perspective—an Almighty God perspective—eternal, not temporal; infinite, not finite.

Paul, in I Corinthians 15:46, describes one of God's methods for teaching us principles: "first the natural, then the spiritual." God uses things that are present in nature or that occur naturally to teach us spiritual principles. For example, the spiritual concept of resurrection is seen in nature when a seed is buried in the ground, and then it sprouts and grows to be a fruitful plant.[2]

> God wants us to pursue an eternal and infinite perspective!

Picture yourself standing in a wheat field. Wheat, stalks of grain, as far as your eye can see, rolling on the hills, bending and straightening to the breeze, waves upon waves of golden sea. You see no end; it goes on forever. What a perspective you have as your eyes take in that beautiful, rolling sea of grain. But what about the perspective when you bend down and look at one grain on one stalk of wheat? How is that one grain getting along? Is it the right color? Is there a bug on it? You don't even notice those details when you are trying to appreciate the broadest perspective available to you.

The universe provides another, grander picture of perspective. The planet Earth is in the Milky Way Galaxy, one of countless galaxies. Earth is such a small component of our galaxy that it's the size of an atom in comparison to the whole galaxy. The vastness of the universe is a picture of God's being and His power. We cannot see an end or a beginning. We have no idea how big it really is. We don't even have a good grasp of our single galaxy. What we feel pretty good about is what we know about our own planet, Earth. The earth is round. We have maps; we know about ocean currents and air flow. We know about global warming and endangered species. But as much as we know, we know we can never know all there is to know—and that's just Earth. The galaxy? We have only just begun to scratch the surface.

God wants us to pursue an eternal, infinite, timeless perspective. He wants us to *see* the wheat fields, not just the single grain; the universe, not just the planet where we live. He wants us to see His perspective, not just the people and circumstances in front of our faces.

"Be not conformed to this world" (Romans 12:2). If I remain limited to a temporal, finite, and time-bound perspective, I am confined and conformed to Earth and earthly thinking. John, in 1 John 2:15, tells me not to love the things of this world. What constitutes the things of my world—my clothes, my food, my home, my stuff, my career, my causes, my agenda? What do I consider important? How does it look? How does it feel?

"But be transformed." We have a finite, temporal perspective, but God wants us to have a transformed perspective. He wants us to be transformed. The same word that is translated "transformed" here in Romans 12:2 is translated "transfigured" in Matthew 17:2. Matthew is telling the story of the transfiguration of Jesus. The face of Jesus *changed*. His clothes were glowing, and He was conversing with two people (Moses and Elijah) long gone from the earth. This was a one-of-a-kind moment, a hold-your-breath moment. The eternal, infinite, and timeless were actually visible to Peter, James, and John. The unseen was seen by these three earth-tied men. The eternal view was so radical that the three tried to bring the experience into the temporal just to get their minds around it.[3] Paul tells us that as we reflect the Lord's glory, we are being transformed into His likeness with ever-increasing glory. Our essential nature is *changing*—glory to glory, finite to infinite, temporal to eternal, time-bound to timeless!

But HOW? *"By the renewing of our minds."* At the moment of our second birth, the door to the eternal is unchained—the eternal is available. But our view, our perspective, is so limited. Our minds just can't seem to break through. We are like Peter, James, and John. Instead of entering into the eternal—seeing with eternal perspective—we corral the infinite into a finite context where our minds—our unrenewed, untransformed minds—can handle it. However, our minds don't have to remain tethered to the earth side of that door. Our minds are renewable—piece by piece, thought by thought, perception by perception—an awakening. As each segment of our minds is renewed, it bursts into the brightness—the glory—of eternity!

What are the things of this world that are the most enticing to you?

Is it difficult for you to embrace the reality of the unseen? If so, why?

What does your process of mind renewal look like?

As our bodies, our finite houses, are eroding; our inner beings, our minds and our spirits, are being renewed on a daily basis.[4] As long as we exist in the finite—in tandem with deteriorating bodies—renewal continues to be necessary. As long as our feet are planted on this planet, mind renewal will not be totally completed. However, as we seek God's perspective, we not only begin to see the eternal, what is unseen; we can begin to focus on it. The broader, the more infinite, the more eternal, the more timeless our perspective becomes, the less important the finite, temporal, and time-bound seem to us. We are gaining a perspective of God's mighty hand.

Pete Cook was a man who loved people and football. He could talk to anyone about anything and have a wonderful time doing it. His conversation almost always got to football: what had happened last year, how the team and the coach were doing now, what kind of team there would be next year. When he was in his late seventies this healthy, happy man developed cancer. It was horrible; it had spread too much for any medical methods to slow its progress. As he drew closer to the end of his earthly life, his conversations drastically changed. Football became unimportant. His expression of love changed. Pete wanted to make sure everyone he knew had made a choice for Jesus—he wanted them to be with him in heaven. While he had always had a wide perspective, his focus became centered on the eternal. The finite, temporal, and time-bound had lost Pete's interest. His body was in its final stages of wasting away, but his mind-renewal was in the fast-forward mode.

?

Where is your focus?

What circumstances keep a solid hold on your mind?

Of course, we should not think that God has no interest or concern in the temporal, finite, or time-bound. He created it, we live in it, and He loves us. He cares about the temporal, finite things—the things that affect our time-bound existence.[5] In Chapter 2, we talked about Job's temporal experiences—his losses, his pain, his emotions. What was Job's perspective? How did God respond to him?

Job spent a lot of time exuding intense emotion. He was angry with God about the injustice of his circumstances. He insisted that God was the prosecutor and the judge; and that he, Job, was his only defense. If God would just present Himself and listen to him, then God would relent and fix it all. Didn't God see what was happening? The language Job used indicated that he would like to bring legal charges against God for his circumstances. Almost half the book of Job records Job's verbal defense from every possible angle.

What was Job's perspective in the first thirty-one chapters?

What kind of perspective did Job's three friends have in those same chapters?

However, at the end of chapter 31, Job quit talking. I guess he had said it in all the ways he could; he didn't have any words left. Amazingly enough, his three friends didn't have anything else to say either. They had been unable to convince Job to confess wrong-doing. Of course, Job wouldn't confess because he couldn't see anything he had done wrong,

There was a younger man, Elihu, who had been listening, meditating, maybe even praying during this lengthy conversation between Job and the three older men. He was getting more and more frustrated and angry with these older, and seemingly wiser, men. Why was their perspective so finite, so temporal? While he had been holding his tongue, God had been revealing eternal perspective to Elihu. (Amazing how we can hear God speak when we're not listening to ourselves talk.) When everyone got quiet, Elihu felt compelled to speak to Job.

?

How long can you listen before you speak?

What happens if you speak too soon?

In chapters 33 through 37 of Job, Elihu asked some probing questions, made some foundational statements, and ultimately brought it all to an eternal perspective. Why was Job arguing with God? Did Job really think he could understand what God said anyway? God is the most just, and He is just with every person. Man is at the mercy of God, but God delights in man. God is not toying with man. He is purposeful. He "enlightens man with the light of life"—mind renewal. "Stand still and consider the wondrous works of God . . . With God is awesome majesty . . . He is excellent in power, in judgment and abundant justice."

Following Elihu's introduction, God revealed His presence verbally out of a whirlwind. Now God was going to ask the questions. "Are you going to correct Me? Are you going to condemn Me to justify yourself? If you think you can be God, just save yourself!"[6] Job reeled in awe and conviction.

God's words resonate with almighty power—eternal, infinite, timeless perspective. And Job got it! Job confessed that the things he had spoken in self-defense were beyond his understanding. They were too wonderful, too awesome for him to know. Then Job came to the realization of limited, finite perspective. Job had heard about God, but he had never really *seen* God. He had only been aware of his own life, his own circumstances, his own self-penned script. Now Job's eyes and mind had opened to God's perspective. Job repented of his absurdity of wanting God to fit into the finite perspective of his personal space and circumstances when there was SO MUCH MORE out there![7]

God wants us to look to Him, depend on Him, for everything—not just the eternal—but also the temporal, including food, clothing, and shelter. Look at what God calls Himself:

> *Jehovah Jireh,*[8] "The Lord will Provide";
> *Jehovah Roi,*[9] "The Lord is my Shepherd";
> *Jehovah Maccaddeshcem,*[10] "The Lord your Sanctifier."

We depend on Him for our finite needs—He provides food, clothing, and shelter. He guides, protects, and comforts, and provides opportunity for character change and growth.

But He also calls Himself

> *El Shaddai,*[11] "God Almighty";
> *El Elyon,*[12] "The Most High God";
> *El Olam,*[13] "The Everlasting God."

These names give us glimpses of the eternal, infinite, and timeless God: His plurality, His majesty, His power, His strength, His sovereignty, His supremacy, His unchangeableness, and His inexhaustibleness.

God's very essence also provides a way for us to make that leap from a temporal perspective to the eternal perspective:

> *Yahweh Tsidkenu,*[14] "The Lord our Righteousness";
> *Yahweh Shalom,*[15] "The Lord our Peace";
> *Yahweh Sabbaoth,*[16] "The Lord of Hosts."

We can put on that spotless robe of Jesus' righteousness;[17] have the "peace that passes all understanding"[18] in the middle of chaos, injustice, and tragedy; and know that "those who are with us" (the angelic hosts) are "greater than those who are with them."[19] God is in the atom and the grain, and God is in the universe. He provides the bridge—The Way—for us to have a personal relationship with Him.

When Job saw God, he *saw* that he was *accepted* by Him. He, Job, a simple man, could have a personal relationship with *God*. At God's direction, Job prayed for his friends, who didn't have enough sense to speak rightly about God. Then God restored Job's temporal, finite space: his possessions, his reputation, and his relationships. [20]

When God restores, it's brand new— always better than it was the first time.[21] Restoration doesn't always look like we think it should. Sometimes God's restoration is only in the eternal and not in the temporal. But if your mind is being renewed, the restoration that means everything is the restoration of relationship to God. Relationship is eternal!

Relationship is Eternal!

What do you wish God would restore?

Is this restoration more important to you than your relationship with Him?

One day a man asked Jesus what he must do to inherit eternal life.[22] Jesus let him answer his own question with the two great commandments. (On other occasions Jesus had confirmed that all commandments were upheld in these two commands.) "You shall love the Lord your God with all your heart, with all your soul, with all your strength, and with all your mind, and your neighbor as yourself."[23] Relationship— relationship with God and relationship with our fellow man. Eternal, infinite, timeless perspective is about relationship!

Jesus told the story of the Good Samaritan to illustrate man-to-man relationship.[24] You know the story—a man had been robbed, beaten, and left to die on a dangerous road between Jerusalem and Jericho. First, a priest traveling down the road saw the man and moved to the far side of the road to pass by him. Then a Levite passed by, moving to the other side of the road as well. What were these two men thinking? "I've got to be at the Temple. I've got places to go and people to see—my ministry. I remember the last time this happened—I might get hurt, robbed. This isn't my job, not my gifting, I don't have grace for this."

Whatever the priest and the Levite were thinking, I'm pretty sure that, "It's all about me" was part of it—temporal, finite, and time-bound perspective. *They were not living to love (relationship); they were living to protect themselves from dying (circumstances).*

Only the Samaritan was living in the Present Moment with God. Abundant Life was there for him. Like Jesus, he participated and cooperated with what the Father was doing without being overwhelmed by the possibility, or probability, of consequences. The Samaritan saw his relationship to the injured man in light of his relationship to God.

The more you live to protect yourself, the less life you can have in Christ. The eternal holds limitless possibilities; the temporal is confining and often fearful. Relationship is eternal; circumstances are temporal. Romans 12 continues to say that as we are transformed by the renewing of our minds that we may prove (determine the genuine) the good (the excellent) and acceptable (what God takes pleasure in) and perfect (complete—there is no further advance in excellence or quality) will of God.

> The more you live to protect yourself, the less life you have in Christ.

Without mind renewal, we can't see God's will, His direction for us. The circumstances may seem horrible or hopeless, but the eternal perspective—God's will—is *always* most excellent and glorifying to God!

The balance of Romans 12 gives us guidance in relating to each other. God's priority is relationship. Eternal perspective cannot be had without transformation; transformation is unavailable without mind renewal. Mind renewal is only possible when we choose not to conform to all things temporal (the world). We give ourselves to God for relationship with Him and relationship with those He places in our lives.[25]

> *Therefore, having been justified by faith, we have peace with God through our Lord Jesus Christ, through whom also we have access by faith into this grace in which we stand, and rejoice in hope of the glory of God. (Romans 5:1–2)*

There is reason for rejoicing in the tent of His glory!

> *And not only that, but we also glory in tribulations, knowing that tribulation produces **perseverance;** perseverance, **character;** and character, **hope.** Now hope does not disappoint, because the love of God has been poured out in our hearts by the Holy Spirit who was given to us. (Romans 5:3–5, my emphasis)*

?

Do you see yourself as the priest, the Levite, or the Samaritan?

Do you consistently seize "present moment" opportunities?

His glory! The awareness of Who He is!
The Great I AM!
Eternal, Infinite, and Timeless!

8 Forgive

Genesis doesn't give us any insight on when or how Joseph came to forgive each person whose words or actions had a negative impact on his life. Maybe after he shared his dreams with his family, he spent time alone processing his rejection and scorn. Maybe God reassured Joseph of the source of those dreams and gave him the grace to forgive those offenses quickly. Perhaps as Joseph traveled in the Ishmaelite caravan, his relationship to God was developing and maturing as he was coming to forgiveness. God might have been the only one on that trip with whom Joseph could talk.

We know that by the time Joseph was purchased by Potiphar, the boy who was the object of ridicule and hate was becoming a man of grace and blessing—a man of eternal perspective. Joseph made a choice to be used by God wherever he was. His decision was evidenced by the success of those he served. Joseph's relationship with God opened the door to limitless perspective, and that perspective made forgiveness for all those words and acts of betrayal non-negotiable. Joseph realized that every circumstance was an assignment.

Forgiveness—how can I get there and stay there? What if the same thing keeps happening over and over again? Is God requiring something of me that I am simply unable to do? Or, am I so hurt and so scarred that I just don't want to forgive? Has the offending party robbed me of so much—my past, my present, my future—that I don't want to give anything, especially not forgiveness?

> Without eternal perspective I cannot forgive, and unless I forgive, I cannot have eternal perspective.

Without eternal perspective I cannot forgive, and unless I forgive, I have no awareness of eternal perspective. When I persist in unforgiveness, every circumstance feels like it is gouging my wounds. Then I certainly don't experience any circumstance as an assignment. When my circumstances control my life—"I'm a victim, life isn't fair, if only . . . ." I am unforgiving, and I am imprisoning myself. My offender is not receiving nearly the punishment that I am doling out to myself. I once heard someone say that unforgiveness is like "taking a spoonful of poison every day, hoping the other person will die."

Most of us have acquired or maybe inherited some wrong information about forgiveness, and the enemy has used that information against us to keep us in the unforgiveness jail. My father would occasionally through the years admit that though he had forgiven his sibling for offenses, he had not forgotten. Consequently, he surmised that he must not have genuinely forgiven. Maybe that's a saying to which you have adhered, "just forgive and forget." I am so thankful that God forgets, obliterates, eradicates, my sin—and yours. But, is He expecting that of me?????

Is unforgiveness killing you?

Are you in the unforgiveness jail?

If so, what is keeping you there?

I believe that Joseph had already forgiven his brothers before they made their surprise visit to Egypt. However, although the spiritual transaction of forgiveness had probably taken place, there was some emotional residue. He cried, he threw them in jail, he held one brother hostage, he tricked them, he sobbed. Joseph still had the accumulated emotion of the betrayal of his youth. He had not forgotten.

Is it possible to have forgiven someone, and yet still have negative emotions, or to still be affected by difficult ongoing consequences?

What is an example in your life?

In Deuteronomy 25:17, God commands the Israelites to "Remember what the Amalekites did to you." In the next chapter, God instructs the Israelites to recount all of the afflictions they had received at the hand of the Egyptians—those Egyptians who only a few hundred years earlier had provided food, clothing, and shelter generously to Joseph's family, the Israelites. Did God want the Israelites to harbor unforgiveness for the atrocities of the Amalekites and the Egyptians? No! God was directing them to *review* where they had been, and where they were going with an eternal perspective. God, "with a mighty hand and outstretched arm . . . brought us to this place . . ." and promised "that He will set us high above all nations which He has made, in praise, in name, and in honor, and that we may be a holy people to the Lord our God." (Deuteronomy 26:8,9,19)

Joseph forgave, but remembered. He knew that God had brought him to every place he had been, and then "with a mighty hand and outstretched arm" took him to the next place. Joseph was not a *victim* but a *benefactor* of God's power and purpose, a victor set above not only his brothers, but the Egyptians as well, bringing glory and praise to God. Eternal perspective!

Sometimes God does give grace so that I might forget someone's offense against me; I am thankful when that happens. But memory of an offense, regardless of its consequences, can also remind me of God's mighty hand, outstretched arm, and His love for me. He will save me, deliver me; and I will praise, honor, and glorify His Name. Forgiveness is not about what someone did to me. It's about what God is doing and will do not only in the circumstances, but also, most importantly, in my relationship with Him. Forgiveness is not about the past. It's about the present and future.

What about relationship with my offender? If I forgive, does the relationship automatically return to the way it was before the transgression or affront? No, the relationship will always be different. The offense and its consequences become part of the fabric of the relationship. The offender frequently just wants the victim to "forgive and put it all behind." Usually, that means "let's just pretend it never happened." Offenses, consequences, repentance (or the absence of repentance), and forgiveness (or the absence of forgiveness) are part of every relationship, either strengthening or eroding it.

Joseph never had a great relationship with his brothers. They resented and hated him. He longed for acceptance from them. He pestered and irritated them; they plotted revenge. When the "dance," the offending and posturing, was over, Joseph was forgiving and kind to his brothers. He made sure they had everything they needed, not just enough to survive, but an abundance.[1]

Perhaps Joseph saw his brothers occasionally when he went to visit his dad. Maybe they saw him coming and went the other way. Although they all mourned together when their father Jacob died, and they corporately traveled on the long journey to bury him, they might not have been that "together."[2] The next move by the brothers indicated that their relationship with Joseph had not been strengthened over time.

When Jacob had been buried, and everyone was back in Egypt, fear began to build in Joseph's brothers. Was it the guilt that fostered the fear? Was it each man's earthly, shortened perspective—each one's limited relationship with God? They began to talk together, their fear mounting with each conversation. They came to the conclusion that Joseph's kindness would surely come to an abrupt end. They knew that they had experienced the brunt of Joseph's emotion years earlier when they came to Egypt for food. They were also very aware that he never fully repaid them for the horrible things they did to him. So they panicked as they thought, "Maybe now—Daddy is gone; Joseph has no reason to be kind any longer. What will he do to us? What are we going to do?"

Joseph's anxious brothers devised a plan.[3] They sent messengers to Joseph to play the "Daddy" card. The messengers said, "Before your father died, his last request was to tell you that he wanted you to forgive your brothers. What they did was evil, but they serve the same God you serve so please forgive them."

Joseph cried. He wept. Could it be that after all this time, they still did not know him? They didn't know what he was about? They could not comprehend Joseph's fear of God—his relationship with the Almighty—that came with eternal perspective.

Then the brothers arrived, hoping that the words of the messengers had softened Joseph. They *bowed* down again (can you believe it?) and offered themselves as servants to Joseph. Joseph responded in kindness, telling them not to be afraid of him. After all, he asked, "Am I in the place of God?"[4] He was telling them that their sin was between them and God. It was not Joseph's job to punish or take vengeance for sin. They needed to seek forgiveness from God.

Joseph then went on to say that his response to their offense against him was between him and God, and he had chosen eternal perspective.

The brothers meant for their actions to harm, "but God meant it for good."[5] God used Joseph's response to their evil, his acceptance of assignment, his confidence in God's mighty hand and outstretched arm, his desire for eternal perspective, to save many people from starvation.

Joseph did not tell his brothers, "Oh, that's okay. I had a few hard years, but everything turned out okay." He did not minimize their sin. To do so would have trivialized God's mighty hand, and perhaps would have short-circuited what God was doing in the hearts of those men. Their sin was real, and it was a matter they needed to take up with God.

> Throwing a small, general blanket of forgiveness over an offense laden with consequences just doesn't work. You must count the cost.
>
> Do you have a situation that you need to "count the cost" before you can forgive?

Joseph reassured his brothers again not to be afraid. He promised care, gave comfort, and spoke kindly. Perhaps the relationship between Joseph and his brothers improved after this encounter. Maybe the confrontation of the brothers with their fear and with Joseph provided a vehicle to turn things around.

It's important to remember that though God mandates forgiveness, He does not want us to devalue ourselves by minimizing the effects of sin's consequences; or out of a misunderstanding of forgiveness, put ourselves back in harm's way. He never requires us to trust the untrustworthy or to consent to victimization. To do so narrows our perspective. We might miss the move of the mighty hand of God. Could God have accomplished His purposes without Joseph's cooperation? Certainly! But Joseph would have been left a resentful, bitter, broken man—a victim with no choice and no hope, surrounded by starving people, and starving himself.

What if Joseph had allowed his assignments to be sabotaged by the absence of apology from those who hurt him? I think of the times, especially when I was in high school, when someone hurt my feelings or said something about me to someone else. I always had the "I'll show them" attitude, which for me meant I'll just ignore you, not look at you, certainly not talk to you. The relationship didn't just disappear; it really took more of my attention and my emotion to ignore the painful relationship. I could never be in the present moment. I rationalized, "If that person would just realize what he had done, the offense he had committed, and apologize to me. Then I could get on with my life."

What if Jesus' destiny had been put on hold waiting for Judas to apologize? Although Judas was willing to play the role of betrayer in God's plan, the betrayal was a personal offense against Jesus.[6] The consequences of Judas' offense were huge. Jesus' response to the devastating sin against Him was not between Him and Judas, but between Him and God. The consequences of the sin of another presented His assignment—His eternal destiny.

> **?**
>
> Are you willing to let someone steal your destiny due to your unforgiveness?

A sin or offense committed against you almost always includes a level of betrayal. The temptation is to let your attention and focus center on the act of betrayal and the betrayer. Your responsibility, your only responsibility, is your response. That response is between you and God. Your response, not the offense or the offender—not the circumstances— is the key to walking in the purposes of God. Response to betrayal always involves forgiveness—not trust, not always restoration of relationship, and not a discounting of the consequences for your life.

> If you do not take responsibility for your emotional pain, you will always live as a victim of circumstances.

Joseph did not tell Pharaoh and all his friends how horrible his brothers were, or what they had done. His forgiveness meant that he would not use dialogue about his brothers to influence the opinion of others.

There have been times that I just wanted someone to ask me about a certain person. Then I could tell what really happened, how this person had betrayed me or my friend. What I really wanted was for everyone I talked to about this person to think badly of him, to feel about this person the same way I felt. God has shown me over and over that to sway opinion in a negative way, whether it's true or not, is slander. Slander is sin and indicates unforgiveness.

Do you just want to get even? Revenge? Retaliation or holding a grudge says that God's arm is too short to use the consequences of the sin for your good and His glory in your life.[7] Not letting go of the offense is all about the sin, ignoring the importance of your response, making yourself the "victim god." Your time, energy, and focus fixates on the injustice or wrong done. Vengeance belongs to God, not to you.[8] He is in charge of the offender; you are in charge of your response.

You might think, "I'm in these crummy circumstances because of what Joe Blo did." Will Joe Blo have to do something to make you feel differently? What if he can't? What if he doesn't want to? What if he is no longer alive?

? Sometimes it is easier to forgive someone who has offended me than it is to deal with injustice and offense against my family or friends.

Have you taken up someone's offense?

If you believe the offender is totally responsible for your emotional pain and do not take responsibility yourself, you will always be at the mercy of circumstances or people. You will never be able to live in the reality of your assignment—the race before you.[9] Circumstances are never eternal. His assignment is always eternal.

The response of forgiveness will necessitate a willingness to accept the consequences of someone's sin. Whether you accept those consequences or not, you still have to live with them. It's a heart and attitude issue.

Years ago, God gave me a picture of a merge lane on a freeway with two cars merging. One of the cars was a hot rod driven by an impatient teenager. The other was an old Ford driven by an elderly man. The teen would accelerate and brake, accelerate and brake, trying to force his car into the lane of traffic. The elderly man accelerated slowly, but steadily, until his speed equaled the speed of the traffic. He merged easily between the cars. Then I saw the sign—*Yield!* Yield to forgiveness; yield to assignment. When I fight the consequences, refuse to accept the reality of what happened, and focus on the offense and the offender—I am accelerating and braking, accelerating and breaking, uselessly expending physical, spiritual, and emotional energy.

Unforgiveness is sin![10] Unforgiveness interferes with my relationship with God and is the culprit that keeps the sin alive. Unforgiveness ignores the mighty hand of God and becomes a "god." Unforgiveness prevents present moment living with Him and circumvents assignment. Unforgiveness is a prison of the soul that kills, steals, and destroys!

Remember to ask, "Who is taking the poison?" **If someone has hurt you, and then unforgiveness robs you of your peace and joy— your Abundant Life—he (the perpetrator) wins again.** Are you willing to let that happen in your life?

You can forgive because you are forgiven! Jesus was willing to pay ALL of the consequences for ALL of your sin—physically, spiritually, and emotionally.[11] His body was broken; He was separated from God. He felt abandoned, rejected, and shamed— for you! He felt all of this for your eternal wellness—that you might be healed and whole, united with Him and the Father, emotionally full and well.[12] All you have to do is to accept Jesus' payment of your debt of sin.[13] What a deal! It's such a good deal that you may have a difficult time grasping the offer and the simplicity of acceptance.

> You can forgive because you are forgiven!

Jesus, in Matthew 18, unfolds the story of an unmerciful servant. A man owed a king several million dollars. The economy of the day was very deflated so repayment of that debt was virtually impossible. How in the world did that poor guy rack up that kind of debt? Today it wouldn't be difficult—real estate, investments, diamonds, vehicles, medical expenses. But in that time period, how could someone spend so much money?

Debtor's prison was the debt-collection method of the day. They just tossed the debtor in jail, and hoped that his family and friends would sell enough of their stuff and make enough money to pay off the debt.

But, since this guy owed so much, there was no chance of his being bailed out of prison. His family and friends could have sold all they had, including themselves, and not made much of a dent in that debt. The king, realizing the situation—he was never going to get his money back anyway—had mercy on the man, forgave his debt, and released him from prison. What a miracle!

The debtor understood "out of jail." However, he did not understand that the extravagant debt was totally erased. He walked out, but he did not *feel* free. He still felt the enormous weight of the impossible debt. Did the shame of irresponsibility, immorality, or greed block him from the realization of forgiveness?

With the weight of debt on his back, he came across a man who owed him a few dollars. It was time to demand full payment from everyone who owed him anything. He confronted the man and pressured him to pay up—right now! When the funds were unavailable, out of his own frustration and fear generated by the weight of the debt that he believed he still owed, he threw the man in prison.

Word got around that the man who had been forgiven an unrepayable debt had himself thrown someone else in debtor's prison—over peanuts. Can you imagine how the king felt? He had bitten the bullet, been willing to overlook his gigantic loss. What was this man thinking? His actions were appalling!

Unbelievable, isn't it? I have a debt that is also unrepayable—it is an impossibility for me. Yet God, in His mercy, sacrificed His Son, Ruler of all things, to pay my debt. How appalling it is when I, forgiven of all, do not forgive. If I can fathom the debt that I owe to God and His total forgiveness of that debt, how can I withhold forgiveness from anyone?

Do you really understand God's forgiveness?

Or, do you feel you must do something to earn it?

Think of a time you dined in a restaurant and charged your meal. The waiter returned your credit card with several charge slips. You reviewed the slips to verify the charges. Then you determined which slip to sign for the restaurant, and which one to keep for your records.

When someone offends you, it is as if you get charge slips recording the offense. You look at those slips detailing the offenses against you. Then you count the cost (your consequences of someone else's actions) of the offense and choose to sign for the charges. You give the signed master slip to God. Your signature acknowledges the offense and the consequences that you must bear as a result. But, there is the matter of the duplicate slip for your records. Forgiveness means you take it to the shredder, never to review again. You are not responsible for collecting payment. *Debt collection is God's business, not yours!*[14]

Ephesians 4:31–32 clearly states your choices when you have been offended, treated unjustly, harmed emotionally or physically. Think of these two verses as two sides of the fence. On the wrong side, starting at the end of the verse and working up, is *malice* or *ill will*—hoping something unpleasant, bad, or punishing will happen to the one hurting you. Then comes *slander*—you will report the deed of the offender to others in order to validate yourself and make them think of this person in light of his wrongdoing. The slander leads to *clamor, contention*. At every opportunity you make relationship with this person difficult, not just your relationship, but any relationship that you can influence. Then *anger* starts to take over—you can't think about this person without getting angry. There is no room for mercy, for grace. Eventually, the anger gives way to *wrath*. Your temper may be uncontrolled—*rage* becomes apparent—and it can show up anywhere, pointed in any direction. You become *indignant*—you are right. Being right is now the most important thing to you. You know you're right!

During this process, *bitterness* has begun to grow. Its tentacles penetrate your heart, your very being. Bitterness has taken root. Hebrews 12:15 states that where that root of bitterness has grown, there is *trouble*—you are in trouble. You can't get out of trouble. And, you didn't just bring this trouble on yourself alone. Your bitterness brings *defilement* to many, probably everyone with whom you come in contact.

Verse 32 describes the right side of the fence: Be *kind* and *compassionate—useful, helpful, beneficial*. This person has experienced losses of which you are not aware. *Forgive*—choose to forgive regardless of how you feel. Let the person who hurt you off your hook with no strings attached. You may have some emotional residue that you need to process, but the choice can be made to forgive.

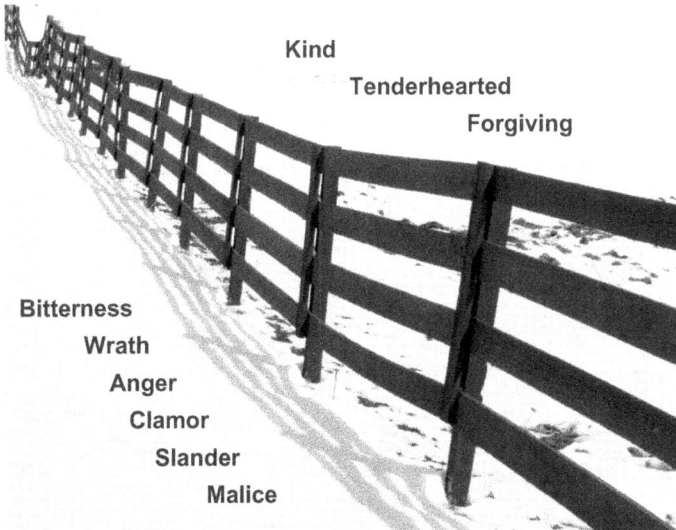

Kind

Tenderhearted

Forgiving

Bitterness

Wrath

Anger

Clamor

Slander

Malice

You can't straddle the fence. If you are unforgiving, you will be on the wrong side of the fence. The consequences of unforgiveness only magnify with time. They are far-reaching, affecting many people. The vice grip of unforgiveness suffocates and destroys relationships.

What about later? You've forgiven—that's GREAT! But, here you are—in the pit of hurt—yet again. Something else has happened; someone else has said something. Or, maybe, someone should have said something, but didn't. It's painful. Your circumstances—they can look or feel like a stone wall that you have just run into or have been flung up against.

With forgiveness and godly perspective, your circumstance is not a stone wall but a segue to Hope!

But wait! As hard as it may seem, with godly perspective, and God's mighty hand and outstretched arm, this circumstance is not a stone wall. Once again, it's a *segue*—a segue into assignment.

Forgiveness propels me through the segue! The segue from hurt to HOPE!

9   *Process*

You have accumulated some valuable information as you pushed through the first eight chapters of this book. You've likely had some revelation—maybe some "aha" moments—as well. Your *brain* is appreciative, but your *heart* still needs some attention. Now it's time for some practical steps.

Identify Your Losses - Loss Chart

If you have not been to a HOPE Workshop or haven't looked at your lifetime losses yet, now is a good time to do that. Think chronologically through your life and list the losses that God brings to your mind. You might want to think in blocks of time (e.g., pre-school, elementary years, high school years, etc.). Don't spend more than an hour on this task. Be aware that any life change brings loss, even if the change is good. Don't try to logically determine if some event should or should not have involved loss, just list it.

Stop here and ask God to remind you of those events in your life that contributed to the unresolved emotion in your glass. Begin your list with your first conscious memory—good or bad. Make a note of each loss event that comes to your mind. Most unpleasant memories involve some type of loss. Consider interactions with parents, siblings, classmates, and authority figures. Consider situations with pets, moves, or school changes. Remember, don't analyze the events, just list them. This is a heart exercise, not a brain exercise. When you have made your list, take a break, and then continue.

Look for Patterns of Behavior

Review your list. Do you see any patterns? Not always, but often, an emotional response will be introduced early in your life, and it reoccurs as one of your frequent responses to loss. Examples include, but are not limited to: feelings of *abandonment, betrayal, anger,* or *rejection.*

> **?**
>
> Do you have one or two emotions (patterns)
> that are frequently triggered in your life?
> (If you are not sure, ask your closest relative or friend.)

Determine Lies that You Believe

Usually early childhood loss experiences include some inaccurate interpretation of events that Satan uses to introduce a lie. The enemy can use this strategy to sabotage your thinking, your relationships, and your future. If you think this may be the case in your life, take some time by yourself, before God, to ask Him to reveal the event where a lie was introduced.

Replace the Lies with Truth

First, focus on the early event and allow yourself to *feel*, really feel, the accompanying emotion. Ask God to reveal to you the lie that you believed in that moment. Can you imagine how easy it is for Satan if you believe a lie early in your life, and you just keep on believing it? He uses it over and over again, year in and year out, with no further effort on his part—the lie becomes so ingrained.

When you have identified the lie, ask God to show you what Jesus would say to you in that same moment—the Truth. What He says to you will never conflict with Scripture in any way. It may be a thought, an impression, or a word picture that is familiar and personal to you. The Truth—revealed experiential truth, His truth in the moment—will free you from the lie and its corresponding emotional response.[1] What amazing freedom!

Other losses in your life have generated emotional consequences or residue. Resolution necessitates verbalizing or communicating the emotion that you still feel from that experience or event. If that emotion disturbs your peace, determines your action, or distorts your focus and perspective, it is unresolved. You may believe that you shouldn't verbalize emotion. That is understandable. Very few of us have been taught to identify and express emotion as it develops. Consequently, unexpressed emotion just continues to accumulate in our emotional vessels, raw emotion leaking or spilling out when we least want it or expect it in reaction to someone or something. What does that look like for you? Anger? Depression?

Are you reminded by God of a specific loss event?

What lie did you believe?

What emotion was established as a response to that lie?

What Truth would God want you to believe?

In Chapter 1, I mentioned that whenever circumstances precipitated emotional spillover or leakage, anger was my presenting emotion. Unfortunately, my anger was an emotion that left hurt, fear, and guilt in its wake. When I was frustrated, misunderstood, fearful, depressed—in fact, when I felt any one of my "feel bad" emotions, I expressed anger. I expressed it freely to my immediate family and closest friends. Occasionally, anger erupted elsewhere, but I usually could keep it directed toward my "safe" people. I accused them. I blamed them. I verbally attacked them. Don't you wish you had been part of that group of family and friends?

Recently, a man told me that his anger had exploded all over his wife. "But," he said, "it had to come out somewhere." His anger with his wife over a particular situation had built and built until his personal volcano erupted. He justified his actions by saying that even his counselor said he had to get that anger out. That might be true, but throwing things, blaming, accusing, yelling or even an "over-the-top" expression of passive-aggressive anger is not only inappropriate, it is wrong!

Directing anger actions at a person or using that emotion to intimidate or manipulate a person is sin. But what about "righteous" anger? Jesus expressed righteous anger toward the Pharisees and the money changers in the temple, didn't He?[2] Righteous anger is directed at evil. I am angry at terrorist attacks, child abuse, and apathetic Christianity. I am offended because of unrighteousness. This anger is justified.

However, if anger is a frequent emotion for you, if your anger is noticeable to, or often directed toward others—righteous anger is not the issue. Anger certainly is one of the emotions God gave you. Anger is purposeful. What is the purpose? God even says that you can be angry, but you don't have to sin.[3] How can you do that?

There is an appropriate way to express the anger—or any other presenting emotion. Maybe you have had a bad experience with a person or persons, and you just keep rehashing it over and over again in your mind or verbalizing it to anyone who will listen—venting. It's certainly true that you need to tell your "stuff" to a safe person. But, if you tell the story over and over to the same person or different people; and your emotion stays at the same level or close to the same level, you are not moving any closer to resolution. You are just rehearsing the events. You are not *identifying and processing* the emotion. You are in essence saying, "This is how I feel. It's the fault of X, and nothing will get any better until X does something." Usually, but not obviously, the stuff you are venting is rooted in old, stuffed emotional residue. How can you find it, expose it, and resolve it?

Review Relationship - Relationship Chart

Look back over your list of losses. Every loss involves relationship—with your mom, your dad, your sibling, your friend, a classmate, a teacher, coach, pastor or other authority figure, a spouse, God, and/or yourself. You need to start somewhere so begin with the relationship that is responsible for most of the unresolved emotion in your vessel. Most often, it's one of your parents, just because they had the most influence as you were learning your view of yourself, of God, and of the world around you. However, if you are struggling with a current significant loss situation—such as a divorce or a death, you may want to begin with that relationship.

Review your relationship with this person, listing the hurts, disappointments, and the pleasures. Include both positive and negative memories to create an accurate picture of this relationship. Again, it may help to approach the review in five-year increments. Stop here and ask God to bring to your memory those events, actions or non-actions, or words that you need to add to your list. If this is difficult for you, answer these questions: When was I the happiest with this person? When was I angry with this person? What did I like best about this person? What did I like least about this person?

You are not critiquing the character of the person. This exercise is not a judgment of action or motive. It is just a method of uncovering the emotion in your vessel that the enemy is using against *you*. Remember, give yourself a limited amount of time to do this work. Don't get analytical.

Use these questions to help you with your review.

What is your first memory of this person?

What specific events provoke good memories?

?

Use these questions to help you with your review.

What specific events evoke painful memories?

What is your favorite thing about this person?

What is the most irritating or frustrating thing about this person?

What do you wish had been different?

Write a Letter

Read the rest of this chapter, then start a letter to this person. You will **never mail** this letter—it is not for mailing; it is for writing. This is for *your* processing. I recommend that you don't use your computer. Some people don't process as much emotion when typing. Remember, this is not a venting exercise or just a rehearsing of the story or events (although you should use the stories and events that you listed in your relationship review to identify your emotion). Writing this letter is very purposeful. Follow the format described below. Be as thorough as possible.

As you write this letter:

• Ask God to show you all the emotions that are connected with this relationship: gratitude, anger, appreciation, love, hate, shame, guilt, resentment, sadness, happiness.

- Write anything you ever wanted to say, should have said, felt but couldn't say—good, bad, whatever has been stuffed, denied, or ignored in your emotional vessel.

- Write how you feel about hopes, dreams, or expectations that disappeared, or were forgotten or stolen as a result of that person's actions or non-actions.

- Write out every specific forgiveness that God brings to your mind. Each forgiveness indicates a wound or betrayal that this person has inflicted, intentionally or unintentionally, knowingly or unknowingly. Many times we have stated a blanket forgiveness for all the hurt that a person has inflicted on or left with us. "God, I forgive my dad for everything." Then, we wonder how Satan can get to us when we think that we have forgiven. The blanket is too small and not specific enough. The resulting emotion doesn't get identified or addressed, much less resolved.

Sometimes it is helpful to think of each wound, incident of physical, emotional, or verbal abuse, hurt feelings, embarrassment, or disappointment as a thorn that has been pushed into your leg. When you throw that blanket of forgiveness over your leg, it is sort of like shaving the tops off those thorns. (You guys, just go with this and pretend.) Your leg looks okay and feels okay until something happens, or someone says something that touches or pushes one of those thorns. Then, it HURTS, really hurts, maybe more than when the thorn was first embedded into your skin.

Do you easily feel the pain of *rejection*, *shame*, *loneliness*, or *worthlessness*? You must pull out the thorn, each thorn, specifically. That means addressing and forgiving each specific wound.

Often, especially if this relationship is with a loved parent, you may be tempted to overlook an incident or words by thinking, "She did the best she could." "He had no idea that his action would hurt me."

Remember, completing this process is about *your emotional response to what happened*. This is about *you*, not about the heart or motive of the other person.

- As you reflect on this one relationship and the specific things that require your forgiveness, you have probably also become aware of some pain or hurt that you inflicted on this person, intentionally or unintentionally. You also need to apologize for anything you did or did not do that might have hurt this person. Be specific.

  When you apologize, you say, "I'm sorry." Some of you may have known that word as an identity—as in "I'm such a sorry person." If that's the case, don't use that word, just write, "I apologize." Sorry is a derivative of the word *sorrow*. When you write, "I'm sorry," you are saying that you are grieved by the distress or pain that the other person is feeling.

  As God brings to your mind your words or actions that have wounded, don't let your sense of being right, or self-righteousness, keep you from being totally honest. You are owning and taking emotional responsibility for your wounding words or actions.

Remember again that this is a letter for you to write, **never** to send. (An unsolicited statement of forgiveness spoken to or read by the person who hurt you will almost always be perceived as an attack.) *This healing work is between you and God.*

Write a Prayer

Every relationship involves God. Once you have written in that letter everything that is in your heart regarding that specific relationship, it's time to write out a prayer. This prayer is for and about the other person. You may need to repent for any unforgiveness you have held. You may need to repent for sins of words or actions you have committed. If this person is living, what would God want you to pray for him or her? How can you ask God to bless this person? In your prayer, align yourself with

God's love, mercy, and grace. If this is difficult for you, ask God for His help.

David wrote a prayer after he was confronted about his sin with Bathsheba. Stop now and read this prayer in Psalm 51. Without your prayer, resolution will remain incomplete.

Who was David's sin against?

What did David ask of God?

Do you think David was emotionally honest?

Before you write your letter and prayer, read the abbreviated examples of letters and the corresponding prayers on the following pages. The "goodbye" at the end of the letter is just signaling the end of this part of the process, not necessarily the end of the relationship. (It's much the same as saying "goodbye" when you end a phone conversation.) Notice how emotions are expressed as well as statements of forgiveness and apology. Remember, these letters were **NOT** mailed!

Dear Dad,

I've been evaluating our relationship, and I have some things I need to say. You have hurt me deeper than you can imagine. Even though you said you loved me, I could see the disappointment in your eyes. I was never good enough. I never measured up to what you thought I should be, or what you thought I should do. Your actions toward me always spoke louder than your words. I hate that you were my father. I am so angry that you were the person I was supposed to be safe with. You were not safe. You insulted me at every turn. You told me I was ugly. You told me I was stupid. You told me I was worthless. You are the one who is ugly on the inside. You are the one who is stupid for not raising me as you should have, and you mean nothing to me. Hate and hurt are so close at this point, I don't know which I feel more toward you.

I forgive you for not being the dad you were supposed to be. I forgive you for not encouraging me when things got tough, and I wanted to give up—especially with the school debate team. I forgive you for opening up my heart to believe the lie of the enemy that I was a failure and always would be a failure. I forgive you for telling me I was ugly, even though I look just like you. I forgive you for making me feel worthless and brushing off my suicide attempt like you approved that I tried because I wasn't worthy to live. I forgive you for being insecure with your position as father. I forgive you for being a jerk.

I am sorry that I frustrated you with my lies and deception—especially where I was after school, and who I was with. I am sorry that I did not respect your authority but tried to fight it at every turn. I am sorry for calling you a jerk.

Thank you for providing food and shelter for me. Thank you for going to work every day to make sure Mom and I had enough to survive.

Goodbye,

Ramona

Lord, I have hated my father for as long as I can remember. I have harbored unforgiveness toward him just as long. I repent for my unforgiveness, and today I choose to put him on Your hook. I know that as I forgive, You will begin to heal me. I desperately need a father so I ask that you bring me one. I know that You are my heavenly Father, but I need one I can touch and hug right now. I pray I would see You more as my Father and learn more about Your love for me, my worth in You, and how You have said I can do anything in You. Thank You for not failing me, for not leaving me, for not insulting me, for not forsaking me. I don't know if reconciliation will ever happen between me and my dad, and right now I don't know if I ever want it to, but Lord, heal me, teach me, and help me to be the woman—the daughter —You have called me to be. I desperately need You. I pray that my dad will come to know You and understand Your love and mercy.

In Jesus' name, Amen.

Dear W *(ex-wife),*
There are some things about our relationship that I need to tell you.
I don't know if you know how much you hurt me when you left. I feel that you treated me like dirt, took me for granted, and walked all over me. You embarrassed me in front of my friends and family. You always tried to look good to everyone and made me look stupid. I am not stupid, and the only stupid thing I think I did was to let you treat me that way.

As much as I want to just hate you and be bitter, there were some good things in our relationship. I was entranced when I first met you. You swept me off my feet. You were beautiful, funny, kind, and compassionate. I wanted to please you. Thank you for loving me and becoming my wife. Our wedding day was one of the best days of my life. Thank you for all the fun times we had. Thank you for the thoughtful things you did for me, like surprising me with a birthday cake and party on my 28th birthday.

I resent that our marriage wasn't important enough for you to work on—that I wasn't important enough—that you didn't love me enough. I am angry that you didn't give me a chance to fight for you—to prove myself to you. I wanted us to travel someday, but that will never happen with you now. You ruined it. What am I going to do? What were you thinking?

It is hard for me to want to forgive you, but this pain is killing me. I know that I have to move forward in forgiveness, or I will never be free from these tormenting demons. I forgive you for not being honest about your feelings. I wish I had known that you were unhappy. I forgive you for not being faithful to me. I forgive you for lying to me about the phone calls. I forgive you for not wanting to have a baby. I forgive you for choosing to go out with your friend instead of spending time with me. I forgive you for leaving me.

I am sorry I wasn't approachable. I'm sorry I put my own feelings ahead of yours. I'm sorry I complained about doing those things around the house that were mine to do. I am sorry I didn't appreciate what you did for us. I am sorry I forgot your birthday.

I still can't believe you left. You are self-centered and hard to please. You listened to everyone but me—confided in everyone but me. Maybe you will have the life you want now. I wish there was a way to do it over, but if you did decide to come back, I don't know if I could ever love or trust you again.
Goodbye,
Dan

Father God,
I hurt so bad. Will I ever feel any better? Will I always feel like a piece of me is missing? Will anyone love me again? Lord, forgive me for not being the kind of husband I was supposed to be. Please teach me how to be the man you want me to be. I ask you to take care of my Ex-Wife. Truthfully, I want her to be miserable without me, but more than that, I want Your will for her life. Please open her eyes to see the truth of what she is doing to herself and others. Please let her find her importance in You. Teach us both the things you want us to learn. Please give me the grace to move on without being bitter, and please help me to continue to forgive. I don't want to be unforgiving toward her. I know it isn't helpful for me. Thank You that You love me. Amen.

Dear Derrick *(husband who died in an accident),*
Why? Why did you have to go? Why did you have to leave that day? I miss you so much! The bed is so big and lonely. Sometimes it is so quiet, I want to scream. I want to scream and yell at God for taking you from me! We didn't have enough time together. We didn't get to do all of the things we planned. I had so many plans and dreams of what our life was going to be like together, and now it is all gone. In a blink of an eye, it is all gone.

I remember when I first met you. You were so shy, I didn't think you would ever ask me out, but you did. Thank you for asking me out. Thank you for asking me to be your wife. Thank you for being a good husband and a good father. Thank you for all the times we were able to laugh together. Thank you for loving me. Thank you for loving God and guiding our family to love Him more. You were the man of my dreams, and I thank you.

I am mad at you for being at the wrong place at the wrong time. I wanted to tell you that to your face, and I'm mad that I can't. I'm angry that I have no one to help me now with the children. It is so hard. It is so challenging. I am so frustrated because I want to sit and tell you all of the things that happen during the day, but I can't! I can't! You are gone and I can't tell you anything!

I am so sorry that all the things we wanted to do when the children are grown, we will never get to do. I'm sorry I made fun of your car. I am sorry that I never got along with your mother. She is difficult, but I will try.

I'm so lonely and sad. I have so many tears—so many questions. So many things I want to say and do. I hope life will not always be this hard. I love you so much and miss you.
Goodbye,
Mary

Father God,
Thank You for bringing Derrick into my life. I am thankful for the years we had together. Thank You for choosing us and saving us. I am thankful that he is with You, and that I will see him again. Even though I know he is with You, the pain is so deep and so real. I pray that You would heal my heart. Sometimes, I just don't know what to do or where to go. Help me to teach our children what they need, since Derrick is not here to tell them things, to father them. Please protect us and provide for us. I don't understand why You let Derrick die. We were trying so hard to do what You wanted us to do, but help me to trust You. Give me strength for today. Restore my life.
Amen.

Stop now and write your letter and prayer. Use this opportunity to express all your emotion related to this person.

Read Your Letter

When you have finished writing, you need to verbalize your emotion and forgiveness. Sometimes this seems unnecessary, but in fact, it is the most powerful action. There is *power* in the spoken word (Proverbs 18:21).

You need to actually deliver, to speak out, the emotion that has been festering in your vessel. If possible, read this letter, face-to-face, to a safe person, *NOT* the person addressed in the letter. In this case, *safe* means that this person will

- keep good eye contact
- listen
- not interrupt
- not analyze your letter
- not criticize your letter
- not touch you while you are reading (touch distracts emotion)
- offer no judgment
- speak affirmation and offer a hug to you when you have finished
- NEVER repeat any of what you have spoken to anyone (confidentiality)

When you have finished reading your letter, get a hug from your listener if you want one. Comfort is good.

Read Your Prayer

Your safe person can agree with you in prayer following the principle in Matthew 18:19–20. "Again I say to you that if two of you agree on earth concerning anything they ask, it will be done for them by my Father in heaven. For where two or three are gathered together in My Name, I am there in the midst of them."

If you do not have a safe person, ask God to be your listener. Read the words of your letter out loud to God. Then, read your prayer. Allow Him to comfort you.

> The power of Jesus Christ brings your healing and freedom!

The power of Jesus Christ is there for you for healing and freedom. All spiritual forces, angelic and demonic, that are present will witness your spoken words. Although it's almost impossible to address all the pain and loss resulting from a major relationship in one letter, the more thorough you are with your letter and prayer, the more healing and freedom you will receive and experience. However, as God brings additional events or losses involving this person to your mind, you can write short, specific addendum letters and prayers to address those things. Be sure to remember that you need to *speak out* those words that you write.

10 *Thank*

You may have noticed that the example letters and prayers in the previous chapter include gratitude—gratitude to the person and gratitude to God. In this chapter, let's examine being thankful more closely because it is vital. I am sure that it's very important because thankful words ("give thanks" and "thanksgiving") appear more often in the Bible than forgiveness words ("forgive" and "forgiveness"). Just as forgiveness brings the power and freedom of Jesus, so does thanksgiving!

Stop and think a minute about those people you know who are always appreciative of what you do, what they have, and what God has done for them. Does seeing their faces in your mind make you smile? I grew up with some of those people in my life, particularly my mother and grandmother. That made a difference in me—I learned to appreciate and thank.

You also are probably around one or two people who respond in an opposite manner—you didn't do it exactly right, and something is always wrong with what they have. They seem to doubt that God wants to bless them. Consequently, they seem to be anxious and complaining most of the time. Who do you really want to be around? The faces look different, don't they? The smile muscles get a lot more exercise in the faces of thankful people.

Several verses in Psalms, Isaiah, and Jeremiah as well as verses in the New Testament, instruct us to give thanks to the Lord, to His Holy Name, to the Lord of Lords, to the Lord of Hosts, and to the Father of our Lord Jesus Christ. I Thessalonians 5:16-18 gives three commands in a row, "Rejoice always; pray without ceasing; in everything give thanks." Whatever your circumstances, be *obedient* to give thanks to God—He is the Deliverer, the Provider, the Protector, the Lover of your soul! Verse 18 continues, "For this is the will of God in Christ Jesus for you." Do you ever wonder what God's will is for you? *Rejoice! Pray! Thank!*

There are times that you need to make a sacrifice of thanksgiving.[1] Maybe you don't want to be thankful. You just don't feel like it, but out of obedience and a desire to bless God, you choose to be thankful. He is worthy of blessing and honor every moment of your existence. Give Him thanks for His creation, for those He has put in your life, for food, salvation, and His comfort. Thank Him for His plans, His goodness, His wisdom, His righteousness. Thank Him for listening, for His nearness.

Psalm 136 is a great example of listing things for which to be thankful to God. His mercy and His love endure forever. This psalm also recounts things God has done—His mighty hand and outstretched arm!

We are continually experiencing and recognizing facets of God's character. Each experience—each awareness—elicits thanksgiving to Him. Continually offer words of thanksgiving just as you continually pray. "Continue earnestly in prayer, being *vigilant* in it with *thanksgiving*" (Colossians 4:2). There will be lethargy in prayer when there is no thanksgiving.

Enter His gates
with
Thanksgiving!

God is blessed by your words of gratitude![2] He has done so much for you, sacrificed His Son for you, wielded His mighty arm for you! He is GOD! Yet, you have a way to bless Him and honor Him and exalt Him by giving Him thanks and praise!

God also does some amazing things in you as you become a habitual thanker. You experience the absence of anxiety—*peace*! When you thought about specific people in your life who were not thankful, did they seem peaceful? I doubt it. When you don't have the peace of God in your life, you have a heart full of discontent, turmoil, regret, and drama. Philippians 4:6 and 7 give us the "formula" for peace. "Be anxious for nothing, but in everything by prayer and supplication with *thanksgiving*, let your requests be made known to God. And the *peace* of God, which surpasses all comprehension, will guard your hearts and your minds in Christ Jesus."

God's peace doesn't make sense to the world. His peace is available to you whatever your circumstances, in any difficulty, in any suffering. You don't have to be troubled or fearful.[3] When you come to God, you trust Him with every need. As you thank Him for His provision, protection, and salvation, your trust in Him grows. Jesus, who is your peace, guards your heart from fear and your mind from anxiety.[4]

In the moments that you embrace His peace, your relationship with Him deepens. "Enter His gates with thanksgiving and His courts with praise" (Psalm 100:4). The gates of His Temple—His *presence*—you actually enter into His presence when you thank Him!

No Emotion, No Intimacy

Relationship with the Trinity—it's marvelous! We have discussed the necessity for emotion in relationship. *No emotion--no intimacy!* Just as He wants to listen to your *feel-bad* emotions, He is blessed by hearing your *feel-good* emotions. Feel-good emotion is ultimately expressed in gratitude. Enter His presence, experience His peace—be thankful!

God's Word also tells us the consequences of ingratitude. If you do not express gratitude to God (and to others) and do not glorify Him; your thinking, your logic, and your motives become empty and worthless.

Without gratitude, your heart is foolish!

Without gratitude, your heart is foolish. There is no understanding in your soul—your mind, your will, and your emotions. Your thinker, your chooser, and your feeler are not working properly. Truth is obscured. If you are not thankful, your thinking is skewed! "For even though they knew God, they did not honor Him as God or give thanks, but they became futile in their speculations, and their foolish heart was darkened" (Romans 1:21). Lack of thanksgiving—ingratitude—leaves you with foolish thoughts and plans. Regardless of your IQ, your education, or your position, without gratitude Godly perspective is unattainable.

God is also blessed when you express thanks and value to the people in your life. When you see a friend with a sweater that really highlights her eyes, don't just think it, tell her. If someone has been especially kind, or your employee has performed a task well, or if the setting sun is reflected in an especially spectacular sky, be quick to express "Thank you," or "Wow!" Or, use whatever verbiage of gratitude or wonder expresses your feelings. Appreciation expresses value and promotes relationship. As you relate to others, focus on what is right, and what is good.

In Philippians 4:8, Paul says, "Finally, brethren, whatever things are **true**, whatever things are **noble**, whatever things are **just**, whatever things are **pure**, whatever things are **lovely**, whatever things are of **good report**. If there is any virtue and if there is anything praiseworthy—meditate on these things." You can only think about one thing at a time. Yes, there are things going wrong; there are mistakes made. There is trouble. Ask God for help, for wisdom to address what is necessary. But, these are not the things to stew over. Meditate, think on the things that are true, noble, just, pure, lovely, and of good report. These thoughts will generate thanksgiving to God and words of gratitude and appreciation to others.

So much *life* is available through gratitude. What keeps you from being thankful? Are you anxious? Do you worry? Do you think you have a right to your blessings? Are you discontent with your circumstances? Do you think you don't have enough? Are you constantly comparing yourself with others and feel you are coming up short?

All of these signal a place of ingratitude. Often being thankful is directly tied to circumstances. You may fluctuate between gratitude and complaint. It is so important that you make a habit to thank God in all things, even in times of difficult circumstances. "Trust in the Lord with all your heart and lean not on your own understanding. In all your ways acknowledge Him, and He will make your paths straight" (Proverbs 3:5-6). Trust God. Count on Him to make a way for you. When you depend on your own wisdom and ability, you will be anxious. You will not have peace, and you will not be grateful.

How can you build a habit of thinking and speaking words of thanksgiving? Take *nothing* for granted—your food and comfortable shoes, your job and chocolate ice cream, God's protection and His love! First thing in the morning and last thing at night, express thanks to God for specific people, provision, and whatever He brings to your mind. Thank God for the opportunities and growth He brings through difficult circumstances and pain. Ask Him to increase your capacity for awe and appreciation!

Review your Loss chart.

At every time of loss,
what is something for which you can be thankful?

?

As you review your Loss Chart, ask God to show you
what He did for you.

Ask God to show you what others did for you.

List each specific point of gratitude.

?

Review your Relationship Chart.

For what can you be thankful in this relationship?

Ask God to show you what He did for you, and
what this person did for you.

List each specific point of gratitude.

11 *Complete*

You will witness God's faithfulness over and over, bringing healing as a result of the actions you have pursued in the previous chapters. It's not that God cannot heal without any action on your part—He certainly can. However, many of us have tried for years to rationalize or deny our emotions because they just wouldn't line up with the truth on a consistent basis. We thought that because we had completed the spiritual transaction of forgiveness, and perhaps were even walking in reconciliation, the emotions that we didn't want would just go away.

However, when we hold glasses full of unresolved emotion, the God-intended purpose of each emotion at the time of occurrence gets muddled. It's just all one overwhelming glob of confusion, frustration, rejection, anger, and so on. Jesus has modeled perfectly for us how to use emotion as purposed by God. He recognized, processed, expressed, and resolved His emotion. Not only was Jesus positionally complete[1] in His relationship with His Father (a position we who have accepted Jesus also enjoy); but He also was complete spirit, body, and soul on a daily and moment-to-moment basis. His soul was complete—His mind (fully knowing all truth), His will (perfectly aligned with the Father's will), and His emotions (appropriately responding to and expressing each emotion as it came). Read back over the Scriptures given in Chapter 3 and pay attention to the emotion Jesus felt.

At the end of the day, do you sometimes rehash the events of the day thinking, "I wish I hadn't said that to her. I should have said . . . If only . . . I should have . . . " Jesus harbored no regrets when he came to the

> Jesus recognized, processed, expressed, and resolved His emotion.

end of the day. All emotion had been delivered—at the right time, with the right intensity—to God or the right person. Don't you know that when He lay down at the end of the day, when His conversation with His Father was done, He was enjoying some sweet sleep. There was no second-guessing of His actions, of His words, no script-writing for the next day. *Only Present Moment, Abundant Life, Trust, Love, Relationship!* Jesus is our perfect example of being complete.

In spite of overwhelmingly difficult circumstances, all of Jesus' relationships were complete from His end. He had said what God had given Him to say to the Pharisees, to the leaders, to those following Him, to those harassing Him. At the Last Supper, He washed the feet of each disciple. Not only was this a great example of servant leadership, it was also an intimate time with each man. Imagine Jesus washing your feet—the gentleness, the love, the intimacy of the moment. We don't know what He verbally conveyed to each man, but it was His last one-on-one moment with each one—even Judas. In this intimate moment, His actions were expressing forgiveness to Judas for what he was about to do.

Judas, on the other hand, personifies incompletion—unresolved emotion. We forget sometimes that Judas was chosen by Jesus. The other guys obviously accepted his role as the treasurer of the group. Although we know he wasn't trustworthy,[2] we don't see any indication that the disciples suspected him of any wrongdoing.

Judas most likely believed, as did the other disciples, that the Messiah was coming to liberate the Jews from Roman rule. If Jesus really was the Messiah, then Judas had some expectations. God had filled the Old Scriptures, all of which the disciples were familiar, with prophesies and foretellings of the Messiah. If someone believed that God's Kingdom was political, then those prophesies would seem to confirm that belief.

Look at part of Zacharias' prophecy following the birth of John the Baptist, quoting several Old Testament Scriptures. "That we should be saved from our enemies and from the hand of all who hate us, to perform the mercy promised to our fathers and to remember His holy covenant, the oath which He swore to our father Abraham: to grant us that we, being delivered from the hand of our enemies, might serve Him without fear, in holiness and righteousness before Him all the days of our life" (Luke 1:71–75). Isn't it interesting how all of us, once we have our own agenda, can somehow interpret what God says as confirmation of that agenda? Jeremiah 17:9 tells us how deceitful our hearts can be.

Perhaps Judas initially thought that he was amassing funds for a political coup. As time went on, it became obvious that Jesus wasn't interested in a political kingdom for the Jews. Judas might have become disillusioned, maybe apathetic about what Jesus was doing. His loss of expectation was very disappointing. His leader was Jesus, and Judas was disappointed.

I think that when Judas decided to betray Jesus for money,[3] he thought, "What is the worse thing that could possibly happen? They might slap Jesus around a little." But after all, Jesus had done nothing wrong. They would have to let Him go. Judas could make some money, perhaps to finance a new start in a different place with different people.

It quickly became apparent that the worst was much worse than Judas could have imagined. The High Priest wanted to kill Jesus. He was going to die, and it was Judas' fault! When Judas realized what was happening, he ran to his benefactors. He tried to undo the deal. He returned the money and begged them to let Jesus go. But the circumstances would not change—Judas tried. And when Judas could not fix the circumstances, he became hopeless—so hopeless that he could not go on. Judas killed himself.[4]

Yes, Judas tried to change the circumstances—fix the circumstances—and they just wouldn't fix. But, he did not go to the relationship, the eternal relationship. He could have—Peter did. Peter found himself in some pretty strained circumstances. He had deserted Jesus, even denied that he knew Him—three times.⁵ But at some point, he reconnected with Jesus—maybe he made eye contact with Jesus as He hung on the cross.

A couple of days later, when he heard that Jesus had risen, Peter ran to the tomb.⁶ A few days after that, Peter dove into the water and swam ashore to be with Jesus.⁷ Then following Jesus' ascension, Peter preached the first gospel sermon on the day of Pentecost—more than three thousand people were saved.⁸ Peter went to the relationship. The eternal relationship was made right!

Focusing on the circumstances perpetuates hopelessness. That's what we are doing when we are just venting. In 1 Samuel 18 and 19, David had discovered that Saul was trying to kill him. It was the beginning of years of running and hiding from Saul. It says in I Samuel 19:18 that David went to Samuel and told him all that Saul had done—venting. But David knew about relationship, and he knew about emotion so venting was where he started. But, it certainly was not where he stayed!

?

Is there a situation in your life where you feel hopeless because you continue to focus on the circumstances?

How does perpetual venting keep you stuck?

What steps could you take to move from "circumstance to relationship?"

You may remember that David had an opportunity to kill Saul—put an end to the craziness—but he said he would not, could not, touch the Lord's anointed. Saul, right or wrong, good or bad, wise or foolish, was the man God had anointed for leadership of Israel. David never physically touched Saul, but he continually processed the emotion that he was feeling. His relationship with Saul had to be right from David's end. Psalms 57 and 59 are both emotional responses to Saul's threats, accusations, and wrong behavior toward David. Notice that these two psalms are not venting (just telling and retelling the story, someone's questionable or wrong actions). They are David's emotional responses to these actions. Now, that will get you somewhere!

> Venting is about someone else; resolution is about your response.

Let's take another look at the difference between *venting* and *resolving*. We know that venting is just telling the circumstances—what someone else did or said, or didn't do or didn't say—over and over again. There is no resolution there. *Venting* is about someone else. *Resolution* is about my response.

In Chapter 9, you wrote a letter. This letter was full of your emotional responses to circumstances in your life that involved one person. To empty your cup, you have a few—or maybe many—more letters to write. The only way to empty your cup is to be honest and thorough in completing unresolved emotion in *all* of your relationships.

> You must be honest and thorough in resolving every relationship in order to empty your cup.

Stop here and make a list of ALL relationships that need to be resolved emotionally.

Your list might include the following:
- each parent
- each sibling
- spouse
- each child
- ex-spouse
- any romantic relationship
- friends
- extended family (uncles, aunts, cousins, etc.)
- authority figures (employers, coaches, teachers, pastors)
- co-workers
- anyone God brings to your mind
- yourself
- God

The following examples are letters to some people who may be farther down the list than a parent or a spouse.

Dear Beverly (wife of Ex-Husband),

I have been reviewing our relationship, and have some things I would like to say.

I loathe you. You are the embodiment of everything I dislike. And I hate that you are married to Sam, and you have any say in my kids' lives at all. You meddled your way into Sam's life, you meddle in my kids' lives, you meddle in anything and everything. I have no idea what Sam sees in you, and I don't know what substance you have as a person. I think that you are evil to your core, and I hope none of you rubs off on my kids.

I apologize for resenting you. I apologize for hating you. I apologize for viewing you as a threat to my relationship with my children. I apologize for not being able to love you, my enemy.

I forgive you for trying to rub my nose in your position as Sam's wife. I forgive you for trying to make me look bad at every turn. I forgive you for sticking your nose in where it doesn't belong or concern you. I forgive you for thinking more highly of yourself than you ought. I forgive you for thinking your opinion concerning my children matters. I forgive you for trying to undermine my authority and my position with my children. I forgive you for being manipulative and conniving. I forgive you for lying during the child support hearing.

Thank you for feeding my children when they are with you.
I will never like the kind of person you are, nor will I condone such selfish acts.
Goodbye—I hope for good.
Susan

Father, *Only You can change a heart like mine. Please change it because I am, and have been, a worse sinner than she is. I don't love my enemies. I don't care about her. I don't want to be around her. I don't want my kids around her. But I must forgive her. I choose to forgive her. Quite honestly, I am not sure that You can bring her around to a place where You can deal with her, but You are God. You can do anything. I pray that her heart will be drawn to You. I pray for her salvation because You are the only one who can change her. Bring people into her life who will point her to You. I pray that You would give me a heart of compassion for her. I don't want to be filled with hate. I want Your peace. I ask Your protection over my kids as they are with her. Protect them, Lord.*
In Jesus' name, Amen

Dear Ex-Employee,
   I need to express some of my feelings toward you which are made up of some good (for your family to be well physically and mentally) and some bad (resentment and ill will).
   I regret not firing you when I had the first opportunity. My fear of getting more work piled on prevailed over common sense. I resented your attitude and your dishonesty—never trusted you. I also took the easier road of not confronting you more often because of my personal deficiencies. It was easier to keep you on probation and pass you off to another colleague than to address my problem. I detested having to make excuses for you and gave up on you with no real desire to see you advance or improve. I only wanted to get by with as little pain as possible for me without destroying clients. While I do not want to see you starve or your family suffer, I would like to squash you like a bug in business and run you out of town. I resent myself when I find similar qualities that I detested in you: procrastination, manipulating facts, interrupting, answering questions without listening, and a general arrogance as to how you carry yourself. I am so thankful you are not part of my life.
   I forgive you for your lies and deceit. I forgive you for your lack of integrity.
   I am sorry I didn't confront you. I am sorry that I let you get away with things you shouldn't have gotten away with.
   Thank you for showing up to work when you did.
Goodbye,
Thomas (Former Boss)

Dear God,
How can I say I am a disciple of Jesus Christ and harbor such ill will toward another person, another professing believer? Forgive me for my self-righteous, hypocritical, judgmental spirit. Please extend Your mercy and grace to me and provide a balance in my life where I can address issues head-on and in a

timely manner without getting emotionally off-base and spiritually off-track. Grant me grace that I may not harbor resentment and bitterness toward this Ex -Employee and can be at a place where I can truly pray for Your best for him and his family. Also, Father, grant me the grace and ability to address deficiencies in my own life that I so readily see in him. Protect my heart from hating another person, but grant me courage to address ungodly issues and speak the truth in love. Thank You that You care about me and how I feel, but more importantly, how I should react. Thank You that Your Holy Spirit convicts me of sinful attitudes in my heart and mind—renew them both in accordance with Your desires as set forth in Your Word. Thank You for releasing me from the bonds of bitterness, hatred, and resentment.
In Jesus' Mighty Name, Amen

Dear Pastor Paul,

In looking at our relationship, the Holy Spirit has shown me that I have some offenses against you, and I would like to be free of these things so I can move forward in the life that God has called me to.

I am angry for the way you treated me and my wife. You hurt us deeply when you spoke words of death over us by saying we could never accomplish this new business on our own. Those words were very hurtful and demeaning to us. I am angry because you are arrogant, and you act like you are never wrong. You believe the way you see things is the only way people should see them, and if we disagree we are wrong. How dare you! I hate the way you narcissistically talk about yourself and how great you are all the time. I hate all the inconsistencies that you claim are not inconsistencies in your life, and the way you operate. You like to sweep your own faults under the rug and don't ever admit true wrongdoing, or the things you are preaching but aren't practicing. I hate that you always have something negative and critical to say about other ministries that you don't agree with.

I am sorry for not listening to you, and for not giving you the respect I should give you as someone who has been appointed by God. I am sorry that I didn't fulfill my responsibility to you in the way that was right. I am sorry that you have had a hard life in ministry and personally. I am sorry that I never sought you out as a son in the faith. I am sorry we didn't connect on the level that we should have.

I forgive you for not investing the time you should have invested in me. I forgive you for not believing in me, or believing in what God has called us to. I forgive you for speaking all those hurtful things about other people, including those things about people I care about. I forgive you for the inconsistencies that are in your words and actions. I know none of us is perfect. I forgive you for all the negative and critical things that you have said. I forgive you for being so demanding of us in certain situations.

Thank you for loving us in the best way you could. Thank you for covering us as a family and couple in the best way you could. Thank for you teaching and mentoring us in many areas of life. We have received much from you and are able to walk out life in a strong and mature way.
God bless you in the future,
John Mark

Lord, I thank You because you have forgiven us so deeply and graciously. Now as I write this letter, I pray that Pastor Paul would be healed of his loss and pain that has so clearly affected his ministry and the way he leads people. I pray that You would show him that You love him, and that You are with him, freeing him from fear, comparison, and feelings of inadequacy. Bless him and strengthen him, Lord. Help him to be a great pastor that does great things. In Jesus' Name, Amen.

Almost everyone at some point needs to write a letter to God. Read Lamentations 3 to learn how Jeremiah processed his emotions with God. Use the form below for writing your letter to God.

Dear God,
I'm thinking about my relationship with you.
Show me all the things I need to see.

I'm sorry . . .

I'm sorry . . .

Father, I know that you don't need forgiveness from me. I do choose to let you off my hook for these things that my soul has remembered. I use the word forgive for the choice to let you off my hook.

I forgive you for . . .

I forgive you for . . .

Lord, I am so thankful that you have brought me to this time and place.

Thank you . . .

Thank you . . .

I am your beloved child, and You are the Father who loves me fully and completely. I pour out my heart to You because You really want to hear my words. Thank you for always listening to me. You are the glory and the lifter of my head. I rejoice in You!

I love You,

Dear God, *I have some things that I need to get out on the table with regard to our relationship. I am angry that You let my dog die, a dog that was so sweet and so good. He was too young. Couldn't You have healed him? In experiencing that I realized that I am angry at You for letting my grandmother die as well, I loved her so much. Why would You let her die in such a terrible way?*

I am angry that You have let bad things happen to me and to so many people who love You. They are people who serve You, and what do they get for it? Hardship and troubles! I am angry that You let bad things happen to good people. I don't understand why! You just don't protect us from everything, all the time. You have the power to do so—so why do Your people suffer?

Lastly, I am angry that You don't answer my prayers in the way that I want. Sometimes You don't seem to answer them at all! I am angry because I don't feel like a child of God.

Your Word says that you are just and faithful, loving and kind. So I know that You are those things in my life, but I feel like I need to just say I forgive You. I forgive You for letting my grandmother and dog die. I forgive You for seeming to be distant and uncaring for the troubles that I and my loved ones have experienced. I forgive You for what I think is Your fault with all the hardship and troubles that we face here on earth. I forgive You for letting us go through them, and for seeming to be aloof to our troubles when we are serving You.

I am sorry for entertaining accusing thoughts against You. I know that You are good and faithful. I am sorry for not believing You at Your word that you will make all things work together for good to those who love You and are called according to Your purposes. I am sorry for believing lies about You. I am sorry for believing my feelings instead of Your Truth. I am sorry for believing that You don't care about me as much as You care about someone else, I know You care deeply for me. I am sorry for believing a lie about my identity. I am Your son.

Thank You for Your amazing love for me. Thank You for Your deep care for me and for always seeing me through things. Thank You for having a plan for my life; it is a good and perfect plan. Thank You for being faithful, just, and true, I can always count on You. You will always deal fairly with me. Thank You for calling me Your son. You have given me all the rights and privileges of a son, and I am blessed. I thank You for making me a person who will be transformed and go from glory to glory.

Thank You Lord, because I know that You are always listening, You NEVER leave or forsake me.

Father, thank You that I can tell You anything. Thank You for listening to me and for hearing my prayers at all times. I trust You with all the things that have happened to me, including what is to come. Thank You that You always bring, comfort, peace, and clarity. Your way is the best way, and I commit to You to listen and obey You—even when I don't understand. You are faithful and trustworthy. Thank You for making me Your son and for loving me and for having a wonderful plan for my life.

Your son, David

Be accountable to your safe person to complete these letters.
As you read each letter, you may have been prompted by the Holy Spirit that a personal apology needs to be made to the one you have hurt or offended. If you believe this is the case, discuss it with your safe person. What are your motives? Does anything really need to be said? Will an apology bring more healing to the person you hurt? To you? Answer these questions with the counsel of your safe person, mentor, facilitator, or leader. Your apology *must* be integrious—with no strings attached.

**This is a process.
Stick with it.
The only way to fail is to quit!
It took years of unresolved emotion
to fill your cup.
Praise God, it does not have to take years
to empty it.
Commit to processing each unresolved
emotion—one at a time.**

12 *Maintain*

What would it be like to know you don't ever again have to live with a full cup of unresolved emotion? You can be at peace with yourself, have clean relationships with others, be wholehearted in your relationship with God, and be able to "run the race" without the weight of a full glass. What measure of emotional completion do you want to enjoy on a daily basis?

As we have discussed, resolution is about identifying and processing emotion. While you are working on your letters and prayers, emptying your cup, don't let additional unresolved emotion replace what you have worked so hard to resolve. When losses and accompanying emotions come—and they do drizzle or pour in on a daily basis—identify each emotion and process it.

We tend to more readily realize the need to process loss that is easily identifiable as loss. Remember, however, that any life change includes loss, even "good" changes that you want—*a move, a job, graduation, a marriage, a birth, new leadership.* You may think, "This is great. All my emotions should feel good." Then an emotion comes that doesn't feel so good, and you think, "I shouldn't feel that way. My life is good." So you just stuff and ignore that emotion. *Ignoring or denying emotion just guarantees that it stays around, filling up your cup, ready to spill out when you least expect it.*

In 2 Corinthians 13:9, when Paul prays for the Corinthians "that they may be made complete," the same Greek word for "complete" is also used in Matthew 4:21 for the disciples' mending their nets—an ongoing, necessary maintenance. *Daily* maintenance is appropriately processing every emotion before the end of the day.

Have you ever enjoyed a beautiful, warm, autumn day lying on your back in some cool lush grass, watching the clouds go by? There's a cloud that looks like an elephant—look at that trunk. There's a monster—all hairy and scary! Then you see a princess, wearing a tiara. If you choose to stay focused on the scary monster, you won't see the princess. You'll miss the next thing that comes along.

Our human experience includes loss. It just keeps happening. You can't keep all those clouds in one corner of the sky. Keeping your cup empty requires that you habitually identify and process emotions when they come—Present Moment living! What is going on in your internal world in the present moment? We have discussed other methods, habits we have established for dealing with emotion—stuffing, isolating, anger, TRASH behaviors (refer to Chapter 4). Obviously, identifying and processing each emotion *as it comes* will require some diligence until new habits are established.

So how do you identify and process emotion? How can you keep unresolved emotion from filling your glass again? First, you must ask, "What am I feeling?" Quickly answering this question is a skill that is developed as you consistently ask and answer the question. If your emotional vocabulary is lacking, review the Psalms. David expressed every emotion wholeheartedly. You can always find a psalm that has at least one verse that reflects your emotion.

If you have a presenting emotion that almost always shows up—anger, in my case—then you have to ask, "What am I feeling? Why? Why am I angry?" Anger and depression are often secondary emotions that mask the more painful, vulnerable primary emotion. Maybe in one situation, it will be that you are angry because you were rejected. Keep asking "why" until you get to the primary emotion.

Maybe you can't find the emotion because you don't know what it was that generated your emotional response. To find the circumstance and that primary emotion, you may need to ask, *"Where did I lose my peace? What happened that triggered my present emotional state? When did I last feel peaceful? Then what happened?"*

When you have identified the emotion, ask, *"Why am I feeling that way?"* Your initial answer to this question may be that someone did something, or said something that *made* you feel that way—the circumstances. But, you must go past that. Your emotion is *your* responsibility. Shifting responsibility to another person only circumvents the purpose of the emotion. *The purpose of each emotion is to reveal a belief that you have. Sometimes the belief is based on something true, and sometimes it is based on a lie.*

One of the most frequent sources of emotional pain is memory. Have you ever been doing just fine when out of nowhere comes a sound, a smell, a taste, a view that instantly transports your emotions to another place, another time? You are immediately and thoroughly impacted. You didn't choose it. You didn't intend for it to happen—but there you are.

What about a siren? Squealing brakes? The smell of alcohol? Shouting? Fighting? The smell of cookies baking? A Christmas tree? An "oldies" song? A train chugging down the track? Maybe it's a great memory for you, but any of those memories could be painful for someone else. Sometimes even a good memory evokes present moment pain. Myriads of memories keep floating by. There is no way to turn them off like a TV, or walk away like you could from the cloud watching. They are in your heart and in your head. They are physical memories with emotions attached like U-Haul trailers.

Betty tells us her story:
> When my marriage unraveled several years ago, I had almost thirty-five years worth of memories with which to deal. For the most part, they were good memories. But those memories came with emotions attached. I had to do something with all those emotions. I couldn't just push the "delete" button. I was not cre-

ated with the ability to do that. How was I supposed to go on with this huge chunk of my lifetime just sitting there like "an elephant in my living room?" Not quite a year into my separation from my husband, I came to HOPE for help. Almost immediately, I was able to put the tools I had acquired to the test.

I was shopping at the mall, and a Neil Diamond song began to play over the intercom system in the department store. It was "our song." There was an instant flashback to a time of cooking dinner with my husband and slow dancing to this song in our kitchen. I could smell the mixture of his aftershave and the clam sauce simmering on the stove. A flood of emotions rushed in along with this memory. I had no choice in remembering the event or the emotion, but I had several responses from which to choose.

I could quickly push it away and resist it—*denial*. I could grab the trailer and hang on, letting it drag me around for hours or days on end—*despair*. OR, I could acknowledge the memory, and identify the emotion of that moment. "What was I feeling?" "Why was I feeling that way?" In the memory moment, I felt beautiful, loved, and special. I knew at that moment I was loved. I was beautiful and special to my husband. I allowed myself to feel all the emotions of that memory.

Then I could choose to identify the emotion of the present moment. I was sad—I missed what we had then. I would never be in that place with that person again. That person did not love me, and I was no longer special to him. I allowed myself to feel that sadness.

Then I chose to tell myself The *Truth*. That was then; this is *now*. I am beautiful, loved, and special because God says that I am. My value and worth are not diminished by my husband's choices. My dependence is on God. I feel His love for me. I'm

back in the *Present Moment*, and there are sweaters on sale!
That first big test made a believer out of me. I knew in my heart
that I had dodged an emotional spiral that could have kept me
down for days. The tools are effective then and still are. I use
them all the time. This hasn't always been easy. It's taken diligence and practice to make it a lifestyle. Most of the time, the
memories come, and I process them so quickly I hardly realize
it. My history is part of who I am. I am so grateful for these tools
that have enabled me to be at peace with my past and to live
fully in the present.

Sometimes as emotions come, you figure out what you are feeling, and
why you are feeling that way—God shows you. But you still may not
know what to do with them. You must tell God and/or a safe person.

Journaling is a great way to express all of this emotion, the "whats" and
the "whys." This requires commitment and discipline to the process.
Read your journal entries *aloud* as your soul expression to God.
Remember the power of the spoken word. You can also go back to the
Psalms. Find one that closely fits your current emotions. Then rewrite
those verses, paraphrasing them to be your voice and your soul.

Once you make a habit of identifying and processing each emotion, it
can be done rather quickly, sometimes in just a few minutes. Then at
the end of the day, you can review it with God. The review should
include repentance, forgiveness, and emotional expression.

What works for me is prayer walking—someplace where I can pray out
loud. Find what will work for you on a daily basis. However, remember
that it is productive to keep reading your letters and prayers to your
safe person, at least until your cup is fairly empty.

As you express your emotion on paper, then aloud, evaluate what this
feeling tells you about what you believe. Sometimes it doesn't tell you

anything about your belief. Clouds of depression or other "feel bad" emotion can just be a result of not feeling good physically (low-grade infections, poor nutrition, lack of rest, lack of exercise). Correct the physical issue, and your emotion will lighten. However, if the emotion is persistent, it is usually a response to the belief of a lie—sometimes in connection with something true. The enemy is tricky, isn't he?

For example, someone you love has passed away. You are sad. Your emotion is based on a true event—of course, you're sad. But then you feel additional emotion—maybe depression, anger, or resentment of anyone who still has a mother, a spouse, a child, etc. This additional, pervasive emotion is probably based on a lie: *I will never be happy again. God doesn't care about me. I didn't deserve the relationship I lost*—or any number of other lies.

Ask the Holy Spirit to show you the lie. Then ask the Holy Spirit to tell you the truth. Sometimes He does this through His Word, sometimes through a phone call, an e-mail, a movie, a line from a book, or through godly counsel. ALL truth comes from God and will always be supported by His Word.

You have shared your feelings with a safe person or God—verbally. God has revealed any false beliefs. You've heard God's truth. Now what? You can't necessarily change your emotion, but you can make a choice to make your behavior match the truth instead of the emotion. Your behavior needs to line up with truth—obedience. God always rewards truth-seekers. Truth-seekers are God-seekers. God-seekers are truth-seekers. God is gracious, and your *emotions* will eventually fall in line with your chosen *behavior* as your *beliefs* are changed.

> You can't change the emotion that comes, but you can choose to make your behavior match the truth instead of the emotion.

Don't forget about "feel good" emotions. You must process those, too. ALL emotions are purposeful. "Feel good" emotions all boil down to **gratitude**.

One summer I was out West seeing things I had never seen before. There were some awesome things to see: the Grand Canyon, Hoover Dam, Zion National Park. We took a side trip to see Monument Valley. Wow! Those huge rock formations—God just stuck them out there—I could see them for miles. God brought to my mind the time when He delivered the Israelites from the Philistines by confusing them with loud thunder. (It must have been really loud![1]) Samuel took a stone, set it up, and called it Ebenezer, which meant stone of help—*Thus far the Lord has helped us!* I thought about how in my life each one of those gigantic monuments was an Ebenezer for a remembered time that I could not have made it, could not have gone on, without the Lord's help.

I began to sing a verse of an old hymn I sang growing up, "Here I raise my Ebenezer, hither by Thy help I come. And I hope by Thy good pleasure safely to arrive at home." I am here because God's mighty hand and outstretched arm have brought me this far. And I know—*I know*—that they will get me all the way to my eternal home. Actually, the entire song is pertinent:

> O Thou Fount of Every Blessing, tune my heart to sing Thy grace;
> Streams of mercy never ceasing, call for songs of loudest praise.
> Teach me ever to adore Thee; may I still Thy goodness prove.
> While the hope of endless glory fills my heart with joy and love.

Oh God, align my heart with Your grace. Your overwhelming mercy is deserving of my highest praise. Teach me to always adore You. I will always need You. My heart is full of joy and love because of the hope I have in eternal life and light!

> Here I raise my Ebenezer, hither by Thy help I've come;
> And I hope, by Thy good pleasure safely to arrive at home.
> Jesus sought me when a stranger, wand'ring from the fold of God.
> He to rescue me from danger, interposed His precious blood.

O to grace how great a debtor, daily I'm constrained to be!
Let Thy goodness, like a fetter, bind my wand'ring heart to Thee.
Never let me wander from Thee, never leave the God I love;
Here's my heart, O take and seal it, seal it for Thy courts above.

"O Thou Fount Of Every Blessing"
Robert Robinson and A. Nettleton

I can't make it one day without Your grace. Keep me on a short leash— never able to get my eyes away from You. I give You my heart. Stamp Your seal on it for Your glory!

When I feel, identify, and process, I can choose to act on truth. Then I can experience Present Moment, Abundant Life Living!

13   *Serve*

So, it's not all about you anymore. You have a different, a higher perspective. Now you have some head room in your glass. God has been faithful to show you some tools for your bag to help you finish the process and stay complete. You know how to maintain. You have Hope!

Your higher perspective reveals that your home, your church, your world are filled with hurting people. They need someone to weep with them. They need someone to rejoice with them—you have a mandate. You pray for the lost and hurting to come to your church—but are you ready for them? Would the church be equipped if next Sunday masses of hurting people came through the doors?

In Chapter 1, we talked about Romans 12:15, "Weep with those who weep." From a brokenhearted perspective, I wanted—I was looking for—someone to weep with me. But now, I want to see how God wants to use me to weep with those who are weeping. Isn't it amazing that God wants to use us, imperfect vessels, to express His healing love and compassion? Can you imagine the impact His compassion will have on the world when we learn to express it?

What does it look like to "weep with those who weep?" We want to help those we love, and those God gives us to love, access the *abundant life—LIVE* in the *present moment with Him*. Just as we do in the HOPE Workshop, let's use *LIVE* as an acronym.

L   isten
I   dentify
V   alidate
E   valuate

Are you a safe person? Psalm 25:16–21 is a guide to being a safe person. Are you:

- *Turning to the weeping one? Giving your undivided attention to the one in pain?*

- *Being gracious and merciful, extending the compassion that only Jesus can give?*

- *Being willing to really look at the pain of another?*

- *Keeping or guarding this person's heart? Keeping confidences and considering each person as one of utmost importance to God?*

- *Doing all of this with integrity as well as with gratitude for the righteousness of Jesus that preserves us?*

- *Being willing to wait for God to speak—not just to you, but more importantly, to the person to whom you are listening?*

The most important component of weeping with the weeping is to *LISTEN*. Sarah Young, in *Jesus Calling*,[1] says, "As they open their souls to your scrutiny, you are on holy ground." *Holy ground*—not thinking about what you are going to say. Do you want to pour out your soul to someone who is just waiting for you to pause so he can interject his brilliant insight? Throughout Scripture, it says, "Jesus was moved with compassion for the people."[2] You must continually ask Him to give you His heart for those to whom you are listening. You are on holy ground. Be respectful, humble, honored. Remember, building trust and relationship takes time and lots of listening!

> Are you a safe person, or are you a fixer?

However, you must have appropriate boundaries. Review the definition of "venting" in Chapter 10. You may need to hear the weeper's story more than once, but the story should only be repeated as is necessary to describe and to process emotional responses. You might need to lovingly say, "I remember your telling me about that; you must still be very angry. Let's work on processing your emotion."

Job's friends that we confronted in Chapter 2 followed this "weep with those who weep" directive very well for about seven days—crying with Job, mourning with him, and sharing his pain. But then Job started to verbalize his emotion. They were unwilling to just LISTEN. They didn't agree with what he was saying, which was fine. But they were so uncomfortable with his words, they could not resist the temptation to "fix" Job. They wanted Job to accept some truth, get his act together, and get over it—so everyone could move on. God was not pleased with them.

Russell Friedman at the Grief Recovery Institute teaches, "Grieving people need to be heard, not fixed." It's amazing how many people have never been *heard*. Many people have never had someone to listen, never had anyone who would give them opportunity to verbalize the emotion welling up within. They didn't choose the emotion, and without opportunity to verbalize it, might never see its purpose. Without opportunity to process this emotion, the emotion not only fails to fully accomplish the purpose God intended, it has ongoing impact on their future responses and interactions.

Remember that Jesus was fully Compassion and fully Truth. His first response was compassion.[2] Never in your eagerness to convey truth, rush by or skip compassion.

Are you a fixer? Do you think that if the one in pain can just understand or hear truth, then she won't feel? You hate it when people do that to you, but you are quick to do it when the shoe is on the other foot. Weeping with another does NOT include fixing! Do you feel inconvenienced by another's emotions? Do you quickly offer a solution to avoid your discomfort with the emotions/pain of the weeper?

Moms are notorious fixers. If a child is in any emotional pain, adults can be quick to tell that child what he needs to do to change either the circumstances or his attitude. A quick answer or correction shuts down emotion. It says, "You should not be feeling that way." The emotion continues to accumulate, affecting and sabotaging lives. Not being heard generates either anger and rebellion or guilt and shame, placing more emotion on top of what's already there. The words that were intended to ease the pain have actually added to the pain.

Emotions, especially those in people with full cups, are a wide, wide road—all over the place. Unprocessed, they are like a weight that keeps them stuck. Hebrews 12:1 talks about the importance of laying aside every weight, every unnecessary encumbrance. It is very important to see that the goal is always to make the climb to the truth. But, without processing through the emotions and laying aside the weight, people stay ensnared and can't run the race with endurance. Speaking truth to shut off that overflow of emotion is calloused and arrogant. Even if a person seems to hear it quickly, without any emotional processing, he will be unable to consistently experience that truth. The weight of unprocessed emotion will keep pulling him down. What if Samuel had told David that he just needed to quit saying or writing anything negative about King Saul and just go back to his sheep and get over it?

Proverbs 18:13 tells us that it is foolish and shameful to answer before we have listened. What are you willing to hear? Without analyzing? Without judgment? Without condemnation? Without looks or words of shame? What kinds of things did David say? *He was mad at God. He hated his enemy. He wanted to die. He wanted God to make someone miserable.* It was pure emotion—it wasn't prophecy; it wasn't character evaluation—it was just emotional expression. Can you be trusted with emotional honesty? Are you safe?

As you listen, you become a facilitator of emotion identification—helping the person to IDENTIFY the emotion. Asking "How did that make you feel?" is NOT a good way to help someone. That puts a burden on someone to explain or justify feelings. You may say, "That must have been devastating!" "You must have felt abandoned."

Identify. The person in pain may have so much emotion, he/she can't begin to name it. You may guess what the feeling is, and he may correct you if you guess wrong. That's okay. Since he may not have thought about what the emotion actually is, your guess will encourage him to identify his emotion. Emotion is unlikely to be fully processed, or its purpose accomplished, if it is never accurately identified.

Validate. Genuinely care! Let the person know with your eyes and your body language that you are listening, and you have heard, really heard the emotion. Validation is not endorsement or agreement of what the person may be saying or doing. It is acknowledgment of verbalized emotion—*VALIDATING* the person and the presence of the emotion.

LIV—listening, identifying, and *validating*—builds relationships. *LIV* earns the privilege to speak into another's life when asked. *LIV* builds trust.

Over time, you may be given the opportunity to *Evaluate.* EVALU-ATE—What does the emotion indicate about belief? What is truth in this situation? What does God say? Do not assume—even if you have incredible insight—that you are the one to evaluate. You may see the truth clearly, but that does not mean that you are the evalua-tor. If you do a good job of *LIV*, you have helped the person be in a position to hear God.

Revelation from God
brings
lasting change!

Remember, when God spoke, Job heard, and he was changed. He had rev-elation. *Revelation from God is much more effective than fixing from anyone.* God's truth, hitting the mark, brings LASTING CHANGE!

> Be as available to God for unseen intercession as you are for the visible input of truth!

God may have given you insight or discernment in order to be a knowledgeable intercessor. Are you willing to be as available to God for unseen intercession as you are for the visible input of truth? However, don't assume that you are not to speak into this life if the person has opened the door. Be Spirit-led. Allow yourself to be a healing vessel if God so chooses, but remember—He is the Healer. You want to fear God too much to irreverently tamper with His dealings in another's life. You want to honor God by reverencing His desire and ability to bring His Truth and revelation that will bring about healing and deep, transformational, lasting change.

Instead of setting someone up for the *FALL* (*Fix, Analyze, Lecture,* and *Leave*), you can set them up to *LIVE* by listening, helping them identify their emotion, and validating their pain. God puts us in people's lives to give them a taste of Who He is. God is their source. We are their support. We are not their God!

?

What impact would we have on the world if we truly practiced LIVE?

What impact would we have in the church?

What impact would we have on our families and friends?

In what relationship in your life have you recently practiced LIVE?

Was it easy?   What was the result?

What about your children? If you are willing to spend some time, these skills and habits can become a part of a child's life early, and they can be used for a lifetime.

The *LIV* is just as valid for children as for adults. In fact, if a child cannot express emotion to a parent, it will be much more difficult for that child to have an intimate, emotional relationship with God.

A young, single mom attending a HOPE Workshop picked her daughter up at her dad's that Friday evening. It was a short drive home, but as often happened, the five-year-old almost immediately started crying, "I forgot my Pop-Tarts™!"

Mom said, "We'll be home in a second, and I'll get you something to eat."

"But, my Pop-Tarts.™ I forgot my Pop-Tarts™."

"We have Pop-Tarts™ at home." But then Mom remembered about listening, identifying, and validating. She had skipped all that and gone straight to *E—evaluating*. There were Pop-Tarts™ at home. Starvation certainly would not happen in the next ten minutes.

While Mom was thinking through that, the whining continued, "I want my Pop-Tarts™."

This time Mom wisely answered, "I'm sorry you forgot your Pop-Tarts™."

Silence.

The daughter went to a different topic. Her emotion had been validated; she had been heard. The young mom was amazed at the difference listening and validating had made.

One Friday morning after presenting the *LIVE* acronym to a MOPs group (Mothers Of Pre-Schoolers), some mothers asked specific questions about recognizing the losses of their children. One mom gave the following scenario: Tommy walked in the door from school crying and saying, "I hate Billy." Mom's quick response was, "You are not supposed to hate. You need to love Billy."

Imagine Tommy's insides—all that emotion and nowhere to go with it. Maybe he was thinking, "I shouldn't feel this way, but I hate Billy. He's bad, and I'm bad, too." Remember that not being heard generates anger and rebellion or guilt and shame. Tommy may have added anger to his "hate" and acted out without even knowing the source of the additional anger. He may have felt the shame of "bad" feelings and become withdrawn and sullen.

How could Tommy's mom have walked out the *LIVE* principle? She could have kneeled down, comforted Tommy and asked, "What happened?" And then, *Listen*. Regardless of Tommy's recounting of the events, she could have then offered, "I'm so sorry, Tommy."

Next, *Identify*. "That must have hurt your feelings," or "I would have felt angry, too," or "You must really be sad." Tommy needed to identify how he felt and be able to name it age-appropriately. He might have felt betrayed, humiliated, embarrassed, or rejected. Mom should give Tommy an opportunity to sort out and process his emotions.

Validate. Mom might not have needed to say any words to validate Tommy's emotion. Her body language, touch, and eye contact might have said it sufficiently and convincingly. But the important thing was that Tommy knew that his mom heard his pain, and that she responded with compassion.

A parent's job also includes *Evaluate*. It's part of the training of the child, but not before *LIV*. The little girl who left her Pop-Tarts™ could have done her own evaluating once she had been heard and validated.

Mom wants to teach Tommy to take his emotion, whatever it is, not just to her, but to God. What an opportunity to pray through the emotion with her son. She can teach him to tell God how he feels about Billy and about himself—without shame. She could also use this time to teach Tommy to listen to God. How does God feel about him? How does God feel about Billy? How does God want him to pray about this relationship? About Billy? About his own responses?

Another MOPs mom of three young sons told about her situation. The family had moved to a new city. In the new house, there were enough bedrooms for each son to have his own room. Overall, it was a very good move for the family. However, the middle son, a first grader, had been acting out with a lot of anger directed at his parents and brothers. Mom felt that the problem was the new teacher, who was not as laid-back as her son's teacher at his previous school. Mom's approach to the problem was discipline, but the behavior had not really changed significantly.

At our discussion of loss at the MOPs group, she realized how much loss her children had sustained in the move: friends, roommates, schools, routines, etc. She had never even considered any of those to be loss issues because it was such a "good move" for the family.

She addressed the losses one at a time, on different days, with her son. "You must miss sharing a room with your brother." "It's hard to make new friends isn't it?" "What was your favorite thing about your old teacher?" "What is your favorite thing about your new teacher?"

After a couple of weeks, she reported a drastic difference in her son's behavior. He had been heard. His emotions had been validated. He had opportunity to address and resolve those emotions. He could move on to *present moment living!*

Obviously, every situation won't fall neatly into one of these scenarios. Ask God for discernment—how to listen, how to validate, how to turn your child's heart to God.

If your child cannot express emotion to you, it may be more difficult for your child to have an intimate, emotional relationship with God.

Children can learn how the enemy uses painful circumstances to introduce lies. They can learn to identify the lies as they identify and evaluate their own emotions. They can learn how to take it all to God, feel His love and comfort, hear and embrace His truth. It is so much easier for them to learn this when they are young. Then they have the tools to make it a life-long practice.

You want your child to hear these messages:

- *I will listen to you express whatever emotion you are feeling.*
- *God will listen to you express whatever emotion you are feeling.*
- *As you learn to express emotion, your vocabulary for doing so will increase and come to you more easily.*
- *As you learn that emotion is God-given, you will not feel shamed by it.*
- *You will learn to express emotion quickly and appropriately without sinful action.*
- *Secure in God's love and His delight in you, you will take that emotion and the circumstances to God. You will be free to express anything and everything, embracing the truth of who God is and His great love for you.*

Read the above list of messages again. God wants you to hear these messages for YOU! He wants to use you to convey them, not only to your children, but to those in your church and in your everyday world. Serve Him as you serve others by listening and validating. Point the way to the great love and compassion of Jesus!

14 *Run*

You were born to RUN! "Run with endurance"—*patience, persistence, consistency*—"the race"—*a faith race*—"set before you"—*your destiny.*

In my teens, I cared a lot about winning races. There was so much to think about. The starting line—be sure the blocks were set correctly—just the right distance from the line. If you were right-footed, the right block needed to be further back so that your right leg would push off first. Then your fingers were placed just at the line—not on the line because that would be a foul. As you lifted your body, toes pushed against the blocks, your shins were parallel to the track, and your shoulders were out and over your fingers. Your eyes were focused down the track. Then you listened for the crack of the starting gun. If you took off too eager, too soon, it was a false start—a foul. If you were too relaxed, too late, it was a bad start—the beginning of a bad race. So many things that could affect the outcome, and the race had not even started!

Then, most importantly, was the finish line! The tape stretched across the track waiting to be broken by the winner. As you approached the finish line, you never slowed down until you had crossed it. You made sure that you stretched for that line—your heart crossed the line first. Too many would-be winners saw the finish line, realized that they were winning and eased up only to have a runner behind them, out of their sight, sprint by at the last second, robbing them of their sure win.

Hebrews 11 is an album of heroes of the faith race—men and women, who through challenging circumstances and suffering, grew in eternal perspective. Some received temporal and eternal reward; others only received the best reward—the eternal reward. But for both, faith won.

Hebrews 12:1–2 is an encouragement for each of us to run the race of faith demonstrated by those heroes. "Therefore we also, since we are surrounded by so great a cloud of witnesses, let us lay aside every weight, and the sin which so easily ensnares us. Let us run with endurance the race that is set before us, looking unto Jesus, the author and finisher of our faith, who for the joy that was set before Him endured the cross, despising the shame, and has sat down at the right hand of the throne of God."

In your race of faith, Jesus made the perfect start—His position and timing were perfect. And, He made the perfect finish—strong and true. He WON! Your race of faith had a perfect start and a winning finish by the King of Kings and the Lord of Lords! Now, nothing excites Jesus more than seeing you run the race that He has already won for you! *Jesus*, "the Author," *the One who started*, and "the Finisher," *the Winner*, "of our faith!" Your race, your destiny, has a perfect start and a perfect finish. Your job is to "fix your eyes on Jesus" and RUN!

How do you do that? There are many Scriptures that give directions for running—caring for the widows and orphans, loving God, loving others, hungering for righteousness, loving justice, etc. You need to consistently read and study the Word to know the strategy for today's race. But, let's look at how the *Winner* ran the race. What was His assignment?

In Chapter 1, we realized that Jesus not only cares about you and your brokenheartedness, but also, according to His quoting of Isaiah 61, *He came to heal your heart*. That was a major strategy of His race!

There are some other things in that list in Isaiah 61 that enhance our picture of the race Jesus ran, and consequently, give us insight into our own race. He preached the gospel—*the only really good news*—to the poor. He proclaimed liberty—*freedom*—to the captives, and opened the prison doors for those who were bound. He proclaimed the acceptable year of the Lord.

As disciples, we learn from our Model and Teacher, Jesus. Then, we follow. Praise God, we have the same coach to guide us as Jesus did—the Holy Spirit. Thankfully, we are never alone or unaided in our race—that would be so daunting and overwhelming.

So, how can you model Jesus in your own race? *Preach the Gospel to the poor*—anyone who doesn't know and hasn't received the good news of life in Christ is poor. Be ready for every nudge of the Holy Spirit to speak of the love of God and the redeeming sacrifice of Jesus. Jesus, with His final earthly words, instructed His disciples to "make disciples of all the nations, baptizing them in the Name of the Father and of the Son and of the Holy Spirit, teaching them to observe all things that I have commanded you . . ." (Matthew 28:19-20).

Heal the brokenhearted—Jesus is the Healer, but you are the agent! You know how to listen and bring His comfort and healing. Everyone that you touch either has or will have a broken heart. The Holy Spirit will guide you to the right people and give you God's wisdom and compassion.

Proclaim liberty to the captives and open the prison doors to those who are bound—Jesus is the Winner! Not Satan. Satan captures with lies and deception. Jesus offers freedom with Truth!

Focus on Jesus and race to experience and proclaim His healing, good news, and freedom! Because you live in a fallen world, you will hurt—feel bad—again. You will suffer again. It will sometimes feel as though it is all about you. But you are not starting over! You are learning to identify, to see purpose in, and to process each emotion that comes to you. You now know that God's delight in you is unaltered by your emotion.

You understand that you must strategize in order to keep away from the door where sin is waiting to take control, away from the sin patterns and the lies that trap your emotions and sabotage your relationships. You mind is being renewed. Your communication is becoming consistently more authentic.

Remember—suffering, difficulty, and even frustration require an eternal perspective. You are an eternal being on eternal assignment. God's mighty hand and outstretched arm are always working out His purposes—impacting your life both now and for eternity.

The writer of Hebrews instructs you to run. Run with perseverance—character and hope are sure to follow. Run in the present moment—fully embracing the race. To do so, you must set aside not only your sin, but also the weight of your unprocessed emotions. If you are still dragging that weight like a ball and chain, you may be moving along the track, but you certainly aren't running.

Run—looking to Jesus. Focus—not on your circumstances, but on Jesus. Jesus is at the beginning and the end of your becoming complete. Because Jesus had the perfect view of the eternal, He didn't focus on the suffering and the disgrace of His circumstances—the temporal. The joy, the glory, the vastness of the eternal permeated His every thought, every emotion, every action.

So, don't get discouraged by circumstances. Meditate on Jesus—remembering His perseverance through adverse circumstances—the hostility, rejection, shame, and ridicule. Regardless of the source of your difficult, painful circumstances, *hope is always the eternal result!*

Your hurt had an impact—a ripple effect through your relationships with family, friends, and all with whom you come in contact. But you won't believe the impact—the multiplied waves of impact—your hope will have. As your perspective rises to see more and more of God's purposes for His Kingdom, your hope will increase—hope in the One who delights in you—hope in His glory—hope that does not disappoint! *Present Moment, Abundant Life Living!*

Now may the God who brought up
our Lord Jesus from the dead,
that great Shepherd of the sheep,
through the blood of the everlasting covenant,
make you complete in every good work
to do His will,
working in you what is well-pleasing in His sight,
through Jesus Christ,
to whom be glory forever and ever.
Amen

Hebrews 13:20–21

Notes

Chapter 1, *Hurt*
1 Matthew 5:4
2 Isaiah 61:1–2a

Chapter 2, *Suffer*
1 Job 1
2 Job 1:21
3 Job 2:10
4 Job 2:11–13
5 Job 3:11
6 Lamentations 3:22–25
7 James 5:11
8 Philemon 22; Philippians 1:19
9 Ephesians 6:18–20;
   Philippians 1:12–14;
   Philippians 4:10–13

Chapter 3, *Feel*
1 Matthew 21:12–13
2 Matthew 23:33
3 Matthew 23:27
4 John 11:33–36
5 Matthew 23:37
6 Matthew 16:23
7 Psalm 139:13–16
8 Psalm 31:9–10
9 Psalm 31:11–13
10 Psalm 31:14–18
11 Psalm 31:21–24
12 Psalm 18:19

Chapter 4, *Strategize*
1 Genesis 4:2–4
2 Genesis 4:5
3 Genesis 4:6
4 Genesis 4:7
5 1 Kings 18:19–29

6 1 Kings 18:30–36
7 1 Kings 18:37
8 1 Kings 18:38–39
9 1 Kings 18:41–45
10 1 Kings 19:1–5
11 1 Kings 19:5–10

Chapter 5, *Relate*
1 Matthew 7:1–2

Chapter 6, *Lose and Gain*
1 Genesis 29:31–30:21
2 Genesis 30:22
3 Genesis 37:2–4
4 Genesis 37:5
5 Genesis 37:9–10
6 Genesis 37:18–22
7 Genesis 37:23–24
8 Genesis 37:25–28
9 Genesis 37:36; 39:1–6
10 Genesis 39:6–10
11 Genesis 39:11–20
12 Psalm 105:18
13 Genesis 39:20–23
14 Genesis 40:6–23
15 Genesis 41:1–49
16 Genesis 41:51–52
17 Genesis 42:1–6
18 Genesis 42:7–20
19 Genesis 42:21–24
20 Genesis 42:25–28
21 Genesis 42:29–38
22 Genesis 43:1–15
23 Genesis 43:16–28
24 Genesis 43:29–34
25 Genesis 44:1–20
26 Genesis 45:1–8

Chapter 7, Hope

1 Genesis 40:15
2 John 12:24; 1 Corinthians 15:36–38
3 Matthew 17:4
4 2 Corinthians 4:16–5:4
5 Matthew 10:30; Psalm 56:8; Matthew 6:28–30
6 Job 38–41
7 Job 42:1–6
8 Genesis 22:14
9 Psalm 23:1
10 Leviticus 20:8
11 Genesis 17:1
12 Deuteronomy 32:8
13 Genesis 21:33
14 Jeremiah 23:6
15 Judges 6:24
16 Psalm 24:10
17 Romans 5:17
18 Philippians 4:7
19 2 Kings 6:16
20 Job 42:7–17
21 Ezekiel 36:26; II Corinthians 5:17; Revelation 21:5
22 Luke 10:25–27
23 Matthew 22:37–40
24 Luke 10:29–37
25 Romans 12:1

Chapter 8, Forgive

1 Genesis 47:11 and 27
2 Genesis 50:15–21
3 Genesis 50:15–21
4 Genesis 5:19
5 Genesis 50:20
6 Matthew 26:47–50
7 Romans 8:28
8 Romans 12:19

9 Hebrews 12:1
10 Romans 1:28–32
11 1 Peter 3:18
12 Isaiah 53:3–9
13 John 3:16
14 Romans 12:19

Chapter 9, Process

1 John 8:32
2 Matthew 21:12–13
3 Ephesians 4:26

Chapter 10, Thank

1 Psalm 50:14
2 Psalm 100:4
3 John 14:27
4 Ephesians 2:14

Chapter 11, Complete

1 Colossians 2:10
2 John 12:6
3 Matthew 26:14–16
4 Matthew 27:1–5
5 Luke 22:54–62
6 Luke 24:12
7 John 21:7
8 Acts 2:14–39

Chapter 12, Maintain

1 1 Samuel 7:10–12

Chapter 13, Serve

1 Jesus Calling by Sarah Young, Integrity Publishers, Brentwood, Tennessee, 2004, October 31, 318
2 Matthew 9:36; 14:14; Mark 1:41; 6:34

Caring **Resources**

*Called to bring the hope, freedom, and purpose of Jesus Christ
to the brokenhearted, defeated, and overwhelmed through the
revelation of God's truth and perspective.*

HOPE Workshop

When we come to Jesus Christ, we are not all instantly delivered from the pain of abandonment, the scars of abuse, the fears, the resentments, the heart-breaks—all the unresolved issues that come from living in a world of unfulfilled expectations and broken relationships.

Many Christians battle the defeats, shame, and guilt of inappropriate responses —often kept secret because it has not been OKAY to not be OKAY. It takes time for the Holy Spirit to heal those wounds and restore to wholeness.

The focus of **HOPE** is not only on those in crisis, but rather on the entire church community. **HOPE** concentrates on helping and equipping the saints— including those who outwardly seem to have it together, but secretly struggle, and those who are thriving regardless of their circumstances. Everyone bene-fits, and the whole church is strengthened.

Realistically, everyone is either in a crisis, will be in a crisis, or will minister to someone in a crisis. Therefore, the church must have a compassionate heart, following the mandate in Romans 12 to "weep with those who weep." **HOPE** also provides a wonderful opportunity for outreach by providing a practical community resource for the grieving, overwhelmed unsaved.

Use *From Hurt to Hope* for a book study or use the HOPE DVD set to con-duct a workshop. The workshop can be formatted for a weekend or a weekly study. Order the DVD set from *www.caringresources.com*.

HOPE is a wonderful venue to gain solid insights for enhancing your marriage and family. The principles also apply to many aspects of business. I find the HOPE tools very useful in sales with building client relationships.

C.M.

....

Did I say the right thing? As a nurse on a bone marrow transplant floor, I wanted so desperately to bring comfort to my patients and their families as they dealt with cancer. However, without realizing it, I was losing my health—mentally, physically, spiritually, and emotionally. HOPE taught me life lessons to empty my own emotional baggage so that I could help others and not lose myself in the process.

A.C.

....

I was in a place where I had "done" all I knew to do—read materials, attended classes, sought counsel—but still I came up "stuck." All the resources I utilized up to the point of HOPE were helpful, but it was through HOPE that I experienced effective change.

As a result of learning the practical applications, all of my relationships changed for the better. I actually see the biggest difference in parenting our three sons. I came to realize that HOPE not only changes the course of one person's life; it has the potential to change generations within a family.

D.H.